Contents

LENCH'S TRUST

LENCH'S TRUST

500 Years of Charitable Contribution to Birmingham

Carl Chinn & Dominic Bradley

BREWIN BOOKS

BREWIN BOOKS

19 Enfield Ind. Estate,
Redditch,
Worcestershire,
B97 6BY

www.brewinbooks.com

First published by Brewin Books 2025

A CIP catalogue record for this book is
available from the British Library.

ISBN: 978-1-85858-781-3

Printed and bound in Great Britain
by Hobbs The Printers Ltd.

Foreword

Abdul Malik, Chairman of the Board of Trustees

It's not often you get to be part of anything that has existed for 500 years, not least an organisation with a legacy like Lench's Trust. Reaching 500 years is an incredible achievement for any organisation, yet Lench's Trust remains a hidden gem in Birmingham's history. Despite its deep roots in the city, many are still unaware of the remarkable impact the Trust has had over the centuries. That kind of longevity doesn't happen by accident; it speaks to the generosity of its founder, the strength of the organisation's governance, the dedication of those who have stewarded it, and a mission that has remained relevant across generations.

This book brings to light the fascinating story of Lench's Trust, from its early days in maintaining the bridges of Birmingham to its role in today's social housing landscape. It captures the resilience, challenges, and evolution of an organisation that has continually adapted to meet the needs of its community. But more than that, it highlights the people who have ensured its survival and success. Their commitment has made Lench's not just a part of Birmingham's past, but a vital force in its future

Dominic Bradley, Chief Executive Lench's Trust

When we set out on how we should recognise Lench's 500th year, it became quite apparent that for a big part of our early history we had very little historical information, and that includes our rather mysterious founder, William Lenche. It was also apparent that there isn't much information on Tudor Birmingham generally. After discussions with our Trustees, staff, and residents we wanted to tell our story warts and all, the significant impact we have had on the city of Birmingham, the challenges to keep going, and the controversies too.

Opening our archives, some of which we have stored at Birmingham Library, we felt the weight of our history, it really brought home that we are custodians of a charity at a point in time and the Trust will still be serving the community of Birmingham long after we have gone. In our archives we have lots of information on the last 200 years (which is remarkable in itself) however, for the first 300 years of the Trust our information isn't as rich. That is why we think this research is important, as this book illuminates very clearly that throughout our early history, Lench's undoubtedly was the most significant and oldest charity in the then town and was run by the most important people in Birmingham, the influence of many of whom still reverberates today.

This book helps piece together that contribution. There is really only one man we could have entrusted with pulling together all of this and that is Mr. Birmingham, Carl Chinn, who has done a fabulous job of bringing to life the history of our contribution to the city. We believe his work sheds some light on this important era not only for Lench's but also for our city.

What became apparent when reading Carl's work is that Lench's history is Birmingham's, including the Chamberlains, the Unitarian movement, the origins of the Bull Ring, and so much more and all playing a part in our shared understanding of our city.

Almshouses are considered the oldest example of social housing and were a direct answer, along with the more notorious workhouses, to the rampant urban destitution of the time. The history of almshouses is long and steeped in altruism. They continue to stand as a symbol of security and kindness, and many almshouse charities across the UK continue this important work and support the vulnerable in our society.

The country's current tapestry of almshouses is patchwork at best. Around 1,600 individual charities run 35,000 homes. The number of almshouses may appear small compared to the 4.5 million council and housing association homes, but they are still an important contribution to the texture of the UK's social housing landscape, as well as being an important aspect of the country's heritage (over 30% of almshouses are listed buildings). Pretty buildings aside, in the face of a housing crisis that is magnified in regard to social housing, almshouses offer an essential home to thousands of people in need.

Whilst having this incredibly rich history, it's right that we celebrate it and it's equally important to me that we ensure that our movement remains relevant and useful for future generations and not just a quaint part of British history. Planning is already afoot on our next chapter. Work has begun on a new model of modern almshouse and support offer; we are currently working on multi-generational living proposals; and a planning application is being prepared for a unique EcoPod Scheme to support wellbeing and nature connectivity amongst our city's working elders.

We want to make a commitment that every 25 years we add a chapter to this book to continue to cement the legacy of the incredible work of the trust. We also want to ensure that this information is accessible, and it will be on our website for all to access.

We couldn't have completed the work on our history without significant help, in particular from Charles Gillet our former Bailiff; my predecessor Jean-Luc Priez, our longest-serving member of staff Jayne McGettrick (25 years and counting!); Aaron Mason who trawled through our archives for hours and hours; and Laura Whitehouse who has been a constant support throughout – and of course, Carl Chinn on pulling all of this together.

I hope that you get as much enjoyment reading about our history as we did working on it. All of us at Lench's Trust are looking forward to putting the work in, that hopefully is worth writing about in the next chapter!

Introduction

As a social historian, my early research focused on the poor in England's big towns and cities, with Birmingham featuring strongly. But the deeper you delve into history, the more widely it leads you. The history of women, ethnic minorities, manufacturing, street gangs, and the Black Country have all pulled me in, and all raise many questions of why. Why did street gangs emerge? Why did the Black Country become a crucial industrial centre? Why did ethnic minorities arrive in the West Midlands? Why were women so vital to Birmingham's manufacturing success? Why did Birmingham become the city of 1,000 trades?

It's that last question that leads to the realisation that Birmingham was not a prodigy of the Industrial Revolution. Rather, its growth was evolutionary until the acceleration of the late eighteenth and early nineteenth centuries, and that acceleration happened only because it took off from firm foundations. Those foundations were laid from the mid-1100s when the lord of the manor gained the right to hold a weekly market, but they were built upon strongly by successive generations of skilled and unskilled workers, small gaffers, bigger traders, merchants, and highly successful entrepreneurs like William Lenche.

A man of many parts, he was a tanner, grazier, butcher, and property owner. But he was also deeply religious and imbued with a desire to help those less fortunate. I pay tribute to him for his generosity and foresight in starting the Lench's Trust, an organisation which has helped so many people over 500 years, and I thank Dominic Bradley, Chief Executive & Company Secretary, and Richard Moxon, a Trustee, for entrusting me with writing its history. Arthur Musgrove, Clerk and Solicitor for many years, who compiled a history of the Trust in 1926 to celebrate its 400th anniversary, deserves appreciation, as does Jean-Luc Priez, former Chief Executive, who first discussed with me the idea of a 500th anniversary history in 2015. Finally, I am grateful to Aaron Mason, Systems and Operations manager at Lench's, who scanned many photos and documents for me from the Trust's archives. Other photos are from the BirminghamLives archive, although a few are by courtesy of the *Birmingham Mail* and the Library of Birmingham and are acknowledged as such.

Through researching this 500th anniversary history, I've been drawn into periods of Birmingham's history that mostly have been neglected. In particular,

Tudor Birmingham has been investigated but a little and finding out about William Lenche and his Trustees has revealed the vital relationships of the leading citizens transforming the town into a major regional manufacturing and trading centre. Throughout the centuries when Birmingham had no Council, their successors acted as an important form of local government with the repairing of bridges and roads. They also handed out gifts of money to the poor and provided almshouses for the needy. It was those twin aspects of governance and social responsibility that, from the early eighteenth century, attracted prominent Unitarian families to become Trustees. Their involvement continued for generations, and they oversaw the changing role of the Trust in the nineteenth century as its functions repairing bridges and roads ended and as it expanded its almshouse provision.

Continuity and change have gone together hand in hand since then. After 1945, the Trust moved away from its historic estates and almshouses in the central wards to provide sheltered housing schemes in the outer parts of Birmingham. Yet, as it did so it remained true to Lenche's Declaration of the Intent of Enfeoffment in 1525 that his Trustees should use the income from his estates to distribute in "warke of charyte". Written in English, this was the foundation for the charitable work of Lench's Trust. Fifteen years later, in their Declaration of Trust, those Trustees stressed that they should stand and be seized of the premises left to them "to distribute in works of charity according to our discretion and ordering, where we shall see the greater want". I hope that through this book I have brought William Lenche into a clearer view, along with Lench's Trustees, residents, and officers. It is remarkable that after 500 years, all those concerned have carried on his wish to help those in need.

Chapter 1

Birmingham's Oldest Charity

Tudor Birmingham: Echoing to the Sound of Anvils

Founded in 1525, Lench's Trust is one of the few constants in the succeeding five centuries of dramatic change propelling Birmingham from a small market and manufacturing town into one of the world's greatest industrial centres. Throughout that extraordinary transformation, the Trustees adapted and innovated to meet the needs of less fortunate citizens. Started in the midst of Henry VIII's tumultuous reign by William Lenche's donation of land for charitable purposes, his Trust's income was initially devoted to repairing bridges and roads locally, with the residue given to the poor. From the seventeenth century, the provision of almshouses became an increasingly important feature of the Lench's Trust and by 1881, with its street-repairing functions long gone, it was focused on giving homes and pensions to necessitous women of the 'deserving' poor. No longer restrictive in its approach but proudly inclusive, today the Lench's Trust continues to be a vital force for good in a post-industrial context with its provision of superior sheltered accommodation for up to 200 older people in need.

Yet for all the longevity and importance of the Trust he founded, William Lenche himself remains a mysterious figure, whilst the town he lived in was just beginning to emerge from obscurity. Contrary to popular beliefs, Birmingham is not a phenomenon of the modern world, instead it has deep roots. Yet though people have lived within its bounds for thousands of years, they are anonymous until the tumultuous Dark Ages. Then, around the time of the spectacular Staffordshire Hoard in the mid-600s, the first name appears: Beorma. He and his ingas, folk, founded a ham, a homestead – Beorma ingas ham becoming Birmingham. Though this leader's name is all we know of him, it indicates that he and his group were Angles, an immigrant Germanic people from the Jutland Peninsula who gave their name to England and who were moving westwards from their original conquests in East Anglia.

Despite the apparent importance of Beorma founding one of the earliest Anglo-Saxon settlements in the West Midlands, it didn't come into view until its first recorded mention in the Domesday Book of 1086. Revealed as an insignificant agricultural settlement, it had no obvious distinguishing characteristics or potential for growth. Landlocked and with no navigable river, it was not a defensive site and nor did it boast either iron ore or coal beneath its surface. Valued at merely 20 shillings, much less than the adjoining bigger manor of Aston, it had nine peasant tenants, giving a population of no more than 50. Yet, 80 years later, in 1166, the story of Birmingham's emergence as a great city began when the Norman lord of the manor obtained a royal charter to hold a weekly market at his 'castle', a fortified manor house, on the edge of the modern Bull Ring. A new town quickly developed, with migrants from its rural hinterland attracted by its relative freedoms. Wanting to make money from tolls on traders and rents from tenants, Birmingham's lord held a light touch, whilst there was no powerful bishop seeking his share, and no guilds of highly-skilled craftsmen stifling competition.

The Old Crown in the late 1860s, the mansion house of timber described by John Leland in 1538. Built in the late fifteenth century, it would have been familiar to William Lenche.

By about 1330, it's probable that Birmingham's population was close to 1,000 and though nowhere near as big as Coventry, it was a more important market town than others nearby. Its more prosperous citizens featured in tax records, yet nobody described Birmingham until 1538 when the traveller John Leland arrived. Coming down Camp Hill, he reached "as pretty a street or ever I entrd" – Deritend High Street, or 'Dirtey' as he called it:

In it dwell smithes and cutlers, and there is a brooke (the River Rea) that divideth this street from Birmingham, and is an Hamlett, or member belonginge to the Parish therebye (Aston).

There is at the end of Dirtey a proper chappell (St. John's) and mansion house of tymber (the 'Old Crown' pub), hard on the ripe (bank), as the brooke runneth downe; and as I went through the ford by the bridge, the water ran downe on the right hande (later Floodgate Street) and a few miles lower goeth into Tame, ripa dextra (by the right bank). This brooke riseth, as some say, four or five miles above Bermingham, towards Black Hilles (Waseley Hills).

The beauty of Bermingham, a good market down in the extreame (border) parts of Warwickshire, is one street (Digbeth), going up alonge almost from the left ripe (bank) of the brooke, up on the meane (modest) hill by the length of a quarter of a mile.

I saw but one parish church (St. Martin's).

There be many smiths in the towne that use to make knives and all mannour of cuttinge tooles, and many loriners that make bittes, and a great many naylors. Soe that a great part of the town is maintained by smithes, who have their iron and sea-cole out of Staffordshire.

Almost 50 years later, William Camden formed a similar impression: 'Bermincham' was a town, "swarming with inhabitants, and echoing with the noise of anvils, (for here are great numbers of smiths)". Still, for all that it was the din of hammers and the clanging of metal that struck visitors, Birmingham boasted a wide range of occupations. Amongst them were unskilled labourers, butchers, innkeepers, millers, tailors, carpenters, coopers, bakers, and sellers of hot food, ironware, rope, cloth, and shoes. Most of these didn't pay taxes, unlike the 156 names recorded for the Lay Subsidy of

A Deritend shoeing forge from a sketch made in 1863, one of the many smiths whose predecessors so grabbed the attention of sixteenth-century visitors with their clashing of metal.

1524-25 levied on land and goods over certain amounts. Craftsmen like smiths, loriners, nailors, and weavers and even a servant made up 91% of the taxpayers. However, the overwhelming majority paid only a little and together, they owned merely 50% of the town's wealth. The other half belonged to the elite 9% of taxpayers. Of these, the highest payers were landholders: the lord of the manor, two religious guilds; and two men.

Then came eight men whose rates were based on their goods. They were headed by John Lenche and John Shilton, each with an assessment of 40 shillings. A first cousin of William Lenche, John Lenche was probably one of the two graziers renting land for grazing cattle, whilst Shilton was a mercer, a merchant trading in many things but especially spices and materials for clothing. He would be the first named of William Lenche's 19 friends and associates in the Deed of Enfeoffment, the Deed of Gift setting up his trust. Of the other leading taxpayers in 1524-25, the lawyer Humphrey Symonds was one of the two executors of Lenche's will; two were ironmongers supplying the metal to craft workers and buying back their wares to sell on; one was a scythe smith working in a highly-specialised trade; and the last was a tanner, preserving and transforming animal hides into the leather that was vital for the making of so many goods in Tudor England. That tanner was Roger Foxall, one of the four supervisors of Lenche's will and it was as a tanner, grazier, and butcher that William Lenche waxed wealthy.

William Lenche of Birmingham

The first of his name relating to Birmingham was John de Lenche, noted in a legal document from 1262 concerning the lord of the manor. This was a period when people other than barons and knights were adopting hereditary surnames, a trend especially noticeable amongst merchants, craftsmen, traders, and the prosperous in general. Significantly, last names connected to places provide direct evidence of migration to mediaeval towns because those incomers were identified by whence they came. So, John was of (de) Lenche, hailing from the Vale of Evesham in Worcestershire where there are five villages so called. His type of surname was common in late thirteenth-century Birmingham, with most connected to places now within the city's boundaries or within a 10 mile radius of its centre. However, the pull of the town was shown by a considerable proportion of migrants coming from further west in Staffordshire and Worcestershire, with the Lench villages over 30 miles distant.

It wouldn't seem that de Lenche was pushed to move by poverty as his family were the lords of the manor of what became Rouse Lench. Instead, it's likely that he was a younger son seeking to make his own mark. If so, he did just that as the 1262 source also gives him as a juror at the Warwickshire Eyre, a temporary law court with justices sent out from the central courts in Westminster. Jurors like him were freeholders and usually the leading men in their district. In Lenche's case, this was the Hemlingford Hundred part of the county, covering modern Birmingham, Coventry, Solihull, and much of North Warwickshire.

With no one called Lenche mentioned in the Borough Rentals of 1296 and 1344-45 for Birmingham itself, it seems that John de Lenche was a property owner in Aston, as in 1346, a Robert de Lenche was mentioned in a land document relating to that large and then separate manor. Fifty years later, a William Lenche was recorded as of Duddeston, another manor that would also become part of Birmingham. It's apparent that the Lenche family extended its holdings as the 1471 will of another William noted lands and tenements (buildings) in Saltley, Bordesley, Nechells, Little Bromwich, and Handsworth – all then outside Birmingham.

William's son, John, did even better, going on to own property in Birmingham, where he became a leading citizen. In 1451, he and his wife, Isabella, were registered as members of the prestigious Guild of St. Anne of Knowle. Then in 1483, he was given as of 'Dereyatyende' (Deritend), Birmingham's first suburb, although it was in Aston when he became Master of the Guild of the Holy Cross of

The Guild of the Holy Cross also doled out money to the poor of Birmingham, something that Lench's Trust would take on after the dissolution of the Guild under Henry VIII. This depiction of the Distribution of the Dole by Kate E. Bunce is one of several panels in Birmingham's Town Hall. A prominent artist associated with the Arts and Craft Movement, she was one of several artists commissioned to show important aspects of the city's past. The significance of Lench's is emphasised by another mural by Bunce illustrating its almshouses.

Birmingham. This was the most prominent position in the town. A religious guild founded for the parish church of St. Martin's, it was endowed with property and land by wealthy worshippers. Most of its rental income was spent on maintaining three chaplains to say masses for the souls of dead guild members, both men and women, and on an organist. The remainder went on maintaining the two bridges over the River Rea at Deritend and paying for a common midwife and almshouses for 12 aged brethren. As well as the chantry in St. Martin's, there was a guildhall on New Street, later the site of King Edward's School and now of the Odeon Cinema. The Guild itself was overseen by a master and wardens, all drawn from the most successful men in Birmingham such as John Lenche.

As noted in 1487, his brother, Henry Lenche of 'Byrmyngeham', was the father of William Lenche who endowed the Trust. Deeming himself also of Birmingham, William was obviously an astute businessman making his money through interconnected enterprises which he controlled: buying and grazing cattle; butchering them and selling the meat; and tanning their hides for leather workers.

By the turn of the fifteenth century, Birmingham was a cattle market of regional importance. However, its town was small, huddled around a small space in the Bull Ring and stretching downhill along Digbeth to Deritend. Consequently, most of the manor remained open land in what was called the foreign. This stretched from Smethwick (Cape Hill) in the west to Gosta Green (Aston University) and the bounds of Aston in the east, and from Hockley Brook, the dividing line with Handsworth to the north, and the borders with Kings Norton and Edgbaston in the south (the Middle Ring Road). Much of this area was the lord's own holdings, whilst a sizeable portion was heath (Winson Green). Most of the rest was better suited for animal husbandry rather than arable farming. This grassland for grazing cattle and sheep covered the modern Attwood Green, Ladywood, the Jewellery Quarter, and Hockley.

The cattle trade grew greatly throughout the 1400s and by the Tudor period, drovers from Brecon and Radnorshire in Wales were fetching their stock to Birmingham and selling it at the Welsh Market at the start of the High Street. Graziers bought the animals to fatten them up and either sell them on or have them slaughtered. The Survey of Birmingham in 1553 mentioned about 80 pastures for grazing. These were held by 20 men of substance, several of whom were wealthy graziers dealing in cattle at both the English and Welsh markets.

A generation before, William Lenche was one of them and like others, he sold meat, as in 1520 he was called a 'bocher', butcher. He would have employed someone to do so in The Shambles, that part of the Bull Ring where the butchers gathered. This was probably his servant, William Paynton, who was later recorded as having a shop there and, elsewhere, also leasing houses with crops, barns, and pastures from Lenche's widow.

As had been done for centuries, a drover is driving cattle to the market in the Bull Ring in the early 1800s. In the foreground is the English Cross and in the background is St. Martin's Church. Between them is The Shambles where Lenche would have had his butcher's shop. The Cross and buildings in The Shambles were soon to be cleared to open the Bull Ring, leaving the church at the base of a wide space.

Significantly, Paynton was appointed a feoffee by Lenche in his Deed of Gift and went on to become a wealthy man. In his 1555 will, Paynton left sheep to various relatives, suggesting that both men also dealt in wool and hence cloth.

Woollen manufacture, however, was declining in Birmingham. By contrast, the leather industry was flourishing, so much that it was a staple industry of the town. With no great manufacture of soft tawed leather like gloves and purses or of tanned leather such as shoes, Birmingham specialised in the primary process of tanning. The 1553 survey of the town noted tanneries along Tanners Row, by the modern Mill Lane and Digbeth Coach Station. Located on low-lying ground, they took water from a stream running down to the Rea, across from which was a tannery on Deritend Island. Formed by what then were two courses of the river, it's now the site of South and City College. Copious amounts of water were essential for tanning, a dirty, stinking, noxious trade pushed to the outskirts of any built-up area.

Cattle hides were brought to the tanners from the skinners with the tails, heads, and horns still attached. After they were removed, the horns were used to make knife handles and other items, whilst the trimmed and stiff skins were cured with salt to stop bacteria growing. Then they were cast into a pit of clean water to take away the blood and gore and to soften them. Once ready, they were pulled out and pounded to get rid of the remaining fat and flesh. Next, the hair was loosened in one of three ways: the hides were coated with an alkaline lime mixture; soaked in vats of urine; or left out for months to putrefy. After that, they were dipped in a solution of salt to remove any water and the tanner scudded the hide, scraping off the hair with a dull knife. This was followed by puering, softening the hides to make them supple, achieved either by soaking in a solution of animal brains or bating (beaten) with sticks with animal dung, usually of dogs or pigeons.

With the preparatory stages completed, the tanning began using tannin, a chemical compound derived from certain plant leaves but mostly oak tree bark. This was ground and left to stand with water in leeching pits, with the longer it stood the stronger the 'liquor'. The hides were stretched out on frames and immersed in vats of the liquor. Once tanned, they were washed, rubbed to remove any colouration, and treated with oil such as rapeseed to prevent the skin from drying out too quickly. The skins would then be hung on racks in a dark, warm drying room for between seven and ten days and finally rolled to remove any creases.

Following the tanning, a currier took over, ensuring that the rough, hard and uneven leather was rendered clean, soft, flexible, and waterproof, allowing it to be finished to whatever surface was required by cobblers, saddlers, and other leather workers.

Tanning was a labour-intensive operation, although it's not known how many men William Lenche employed, probably at the tannery in Deritend. What is known is that like most other wealthy Birmingham traders, he bought property to add to that he'd inherited. In 1487, he took over a house in 'Moulestreet', Moor Street, paying the lord of the manor an annual rent of a pound of pepper, an expensive item and signifier of wealth in the Tudor period. Six years later, Lenche purchased an adjoining croft, a small piece of land. This extended to 'lytyll park street', Park Street, where later the Lench's Trust would have almshouses.

Lenche himself lived in the house, partly on the site where the Woolpack Hotel would be built. As well as adding to his property in Moor Street, he bought land near the Bull Ring and in 1506, he gained the 'Calofeldys' (Callowfields) in Bordesley, then outside Birmingham, from a cousin. These, too, became part of the Trust until the site was purchased by Birmingham Council in 1910 and turned into Callow Fields Park, better known as Garrison Lane Recreation Ground.

A drawing of the Woolpack Hotel in 1911, after it was rebuilt in the late nineteenth century. In the early 1500s, this was the site of William Lenche's house.

In 1513, Lenche went on to buy a messuage (house) and lands in Aston, Duddeston, and Bordesley. He followed that with the purchase of a tenement with meadows, leasowes (rough pastures), fields, and other land in Duddeston. This was leased out in 1517, with the document bearing Lenche's seal, a beautifully-formed monogram \%. The principal witness was Thomas Arden of Park Hall in Castle Bromwich, a distant relative of William Shakespeare's mother, Mary Arden.

Lenche's Deed of Enfeoffment, 1525

What kind of man was William Lenche, other than a wealthy and clever businessman? There's no description of him but it's apparent that even though he lived in a religious age, his faith was deep and meaningful. His will of 24 March 1525 began as did all others with bequeathing his soul to almighty God, adding to "our blessed seynt Mary, and all the holy company of heaven". Then he left money to St. Martin's, where he was to be buried, for making his sepulchre; to the priests present at his committal; to the church's High Altar; and to the priests who would pray for his soul thereafter. His religiosity was further emphasised by bequests to St. Mary's Priory and Cathedral in Coventry and to St. Chad's in Lichfield.

Lenche was as faithful to his friends, giving the same sum to each of his five closest, whilst he was loyal to those who'd helped him. The large amount of 20 shillings each went to his servants, Paynton and Roger Hawkes, who also became a butcher and whose descendants were leading figures in Birmingham for centuries. Two other men were beneficiaries. Nothing is known of them nor of Agnes Swapston, one of two women left money. The second was Margaret Varnam who may have been the widow of another servant. What is clear is that she was a well-off butcher and one of only two women named on the Birmingham Tax Roll of 1547 when she was registered for two payments for land.

Having no children, Lenche bequeathed money to each of his unnamed godchildren and the residue of his estate to his wife, Agnes. Apart from this brief mention and others pertaining to her husband, she's lost in the shadows of history, although she must have been a capable woman as she was her husband's sole executor.

Lenche's will also included a small sum for repairing the pavement of Edgbaston Street. Thirteen days previously, on 11 March 1525, his Declaration of the Intent of Enfeoffment made his generosity and concern for Birmingham and its people even clearer. It stated that after his death and that of his wife, his Trustees should use the income from his estates to distribute in "warke of charyte" for the health of the souls of the couple. Written in English, this was the foundation for the charitable work of Lench's Trust.

The Deed of Enfeoffment was issued on the same day as the Declaration but in Latin, the language of law. Giving himself as of Birmingham, Lenche granted to his Trustees:

> … all and singular my lands and tenements, meadows, fields, and pastures, rents and services, with all and singular to them belonging in the parish and field of Birmingham aforesaid, in the county of Warwick, and in the parish and fields of Dudston (Duddeston), in the said county, and in the parish and fields of Aston, in the said county, and in Bordesley in the said county, and in Little Bromwich, in the said county, and in Salteley (Saltley), in the said county; to have and to hold all and singular my lands and tenements, meadows, fields, and pastures, with all and singular belonging to them in the aforesaid parishes and fields …

There were 19 Trustees in all. Carefully chosen, they were men of substance and influence whose tight connections bring into view some of those responsible for building even stronger the foundations for Birmingham's later spectacular rise to

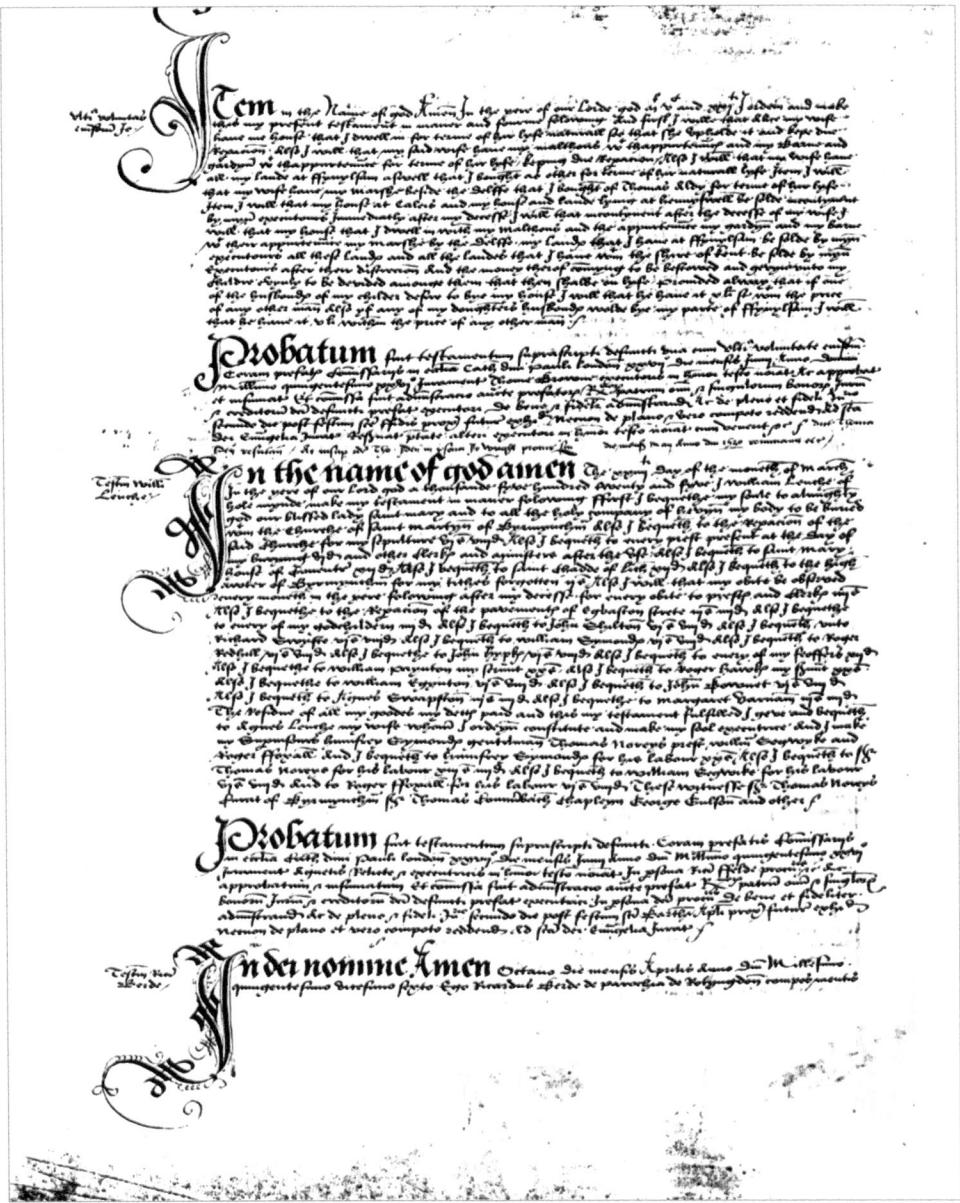

William Lenche's will of 1525.

industrial fame. In so doing, Lenche's deed gives an invaluable insight into the personal and commercial connections of the 'movers and shakers' of Tudor Birmingham, then a town of between 1,000 and 1,400. The first five named were the close friends bequeathed money by Lenche in his will.

They were headed by John Shilton the mercer, probably the richest man in Birmingham and its biggest property holder. His wealth was emphasised after his death in 1553 by the inventory of his goods and chattels. With no such document for Lenche, it gives an indication as to the high living standards of Birmingham's leading citizens. Shilton's large home had numerous items in the hall, kitchen, back kitchen, tavern, malt chamber, great chamber over the hall, plate room, wife's chamber, maid's chamber, high chamber, and two other chambers. Outside there were three tool sheds along with many chattels in wide pastures: 10 oxen; 28 horses; 14 cattle, some with calves; 64 ewes and lambs; 120 hoggerels (young sheep) and wethers (castrated goats and rams); and 14 pigs, little and big.

'On the ground' were eight acres of oats in the hay barnes, land that adjoined the modern Great Hampton Row in Hockley. A much bigger estate was the 29 acres of rye, eight of oats, and four of barley at the Byngas. Later owned by King Edward VI School, this was the farm around Shilton's mansion. The building itself was eventually bought by the banking Lloyds who replaced it with Bingley House. In turn that was knocked down for Bingley Hall, opened in 1850 as the first purpose-built exhibition building in Britain. Today, the ICC covers the spot. As for the Shiltons, they went on to marry into the landed gentry, becoming the lords of Wednesbury and West Bromwich, with one of them achieving the rank of Solicitor-General to Charles I.

Richard Swyft was the second of Lench's Trustees. His family was mentioned in the Birmingham rental of 1296, whilst it was also well established in Yardley, then in Worcestershire. A witness to several other important documents, he was amongst the highest taxpayers for land in Birmingham in 1547. Roger Redhyll was third. Another prosperous landholder, his father left him the substantial sum of £20 in 1522. The rest of his inheritance gives another insight into the possessions of Birmingham's wealthiest men. He received one of his father's three goblets; six silver spoons; a feather bed with all things pertaining to it; a brass pot; 12 pewter vessels; a basin with a laver (wash basin); and a chafing dish (a metal cooking pan on a stand and heated with charcoal in a brazier for gentle cooking away from direct flames). These were all expensive and valued goods.

As supervisor of his father's will, Redhyll was joined by Lenche and Shilton. One of the three witnesses was John Hypkys, who was the fourth named of Lenche's Trustees. It seems he was the father of another John Hypkys, an ox shoer, a highly-skilled man with a home and blacksmith's shop in Winson Green. His prosperity was made clear by his bequests of the substantial amounts of £30 each to his son and daughter. William Symondes was the fifth and last of Lench's friends named in both his will and deed of gift. A cousin of Shilton, he held land

Md, the xj^th day of Marche, in the xvij^e yere & rayne of oure soue/aynge lorde kynge Henry þe viij^th, that this ys the laste wylle & Entent of Wyłłm Lenche, of Byrmyngh'm, vppon hys dede of feoffement, datyd the day of the makynge of this þ)sent wrytynge, made vnto John Shylton of Byrmynghm̃ aforeseide, Rycharde Swyft of the same, Rog) Redhyll, & other moo, as more playnly dothe apeyre in the same dede, of in & appon all he landes & teñte lyinge & beynge w'in the lord-shippe of Byrmyghm̃, Bordysley, Aston, Dudston, Salteley, Nechelle, & Lyttyll Bromwyche, w'in the Cowntye of War-wyke. Ffyrst, I the seyd Wyłłm Lenche wyll, that the seid feoffes shall stande seasyde of, in, & appon, ałł my landys aforeseide, w^t ther apptenance, to the vse of me the seid Wyłłm Lenche & Agnes my wyffe dewrynge our lyvys, & the leng) lyu) of vs. And aff) the decesse of me the seid Wyłłm Lenche & Agnes my wyffe, I wylle þ^t my seide feoffes shalle stande seasyd in ffe of the þ)mysses to ther vse; & pfette of the same to dystrybute in warke of charyte, for the heylthe of the forseid Wyłłm Lenche sowlle & Agnes his wyffe.

William Lenche's Declaration of the Intent of Feoffment, 11 March 1525, written in English and naming only John Shylton, Richard Swyft, and Roger Redhyll from amongst the feoffees.

and property but classed himself as a gentleman, earning enough from rents not to have to engage in trade. On other documents, he was given as an armiger, someone with armorial bearings, a counsellor, and serjeant-at-law and judge of South Wales. Symonds was a powerful and determined man and would be the leading figure in effectively saving Lench's Trust in 1540.

Four other Trustees were amongst Birmingham's trading elite. William Sheldon was a tanner and though not as wealthy as John Shilton, he was a most prosperous man. Dying in 1551, he left over £6 to one daughter towards her marriage; his gown furred with black lamb's wool to one son-in-law; and his best gown to another. Amongst other expensive clothing, he gave his five sons his sleeveless jacket and doublet with fustian sleeves, best doublet of satin, best pair of hose, and best doublet stacked with velvet.

An ironmonger, William King was one of the loving brethren and friends of another Trustee, William Colmore the elder. A rich mercer, Colmore's family would become the most powerful in Tudor Birmingham, recalled in Colmore Row and the adjoining streets. With roots in the Solihull area, Colmore the elder wasn't mentioned in the 1524-25 tax record but was amongst the highest payers in the 1543 Lay Subsidy, exceeding even Shilton and Symonds. He died in 1566 and was remembered by a slab in St. Martin's Church upon which he was shown in a long civilian's gown, with hanging sleeves – each of which had slits at the upper part and through which the arms passed. That disappeared and today one of the oldest memorials in the church is a canvass of dark wood high on the south transept wall. It was erected in 1612 by William Colmore the younger in memory of his parents and shows the 'Grim Reaper' – a seated skeleton holding a scythe.

The oldest of eight sons, this William was a witness to Lenche's Deed of Enfeoffment and benefited the most from the will of his father the Trustee, whose riches were emphasised by his bequests of 100 marks to each of his seven younger sons. A mark was the equivalent of two thirds of a pound and this was boosted by inheritances of property. As for the older Colmore's five daughters, they were each given £100. These were enormous amounts considering that as late as the turn of the twentieth century, the poverty line for a modest family of four was about £1 a week. Colmore the elder also passed on gold, silver, and jewels, and, importantly, added to Lench's Trust with his own charitable bequest.

The fourth Trustee of abundance was William Phillips, whose family had land in Erdington and Bordesley and whose ancestor of the same name was recorded as renting a property from Birmingham's lord of the manor in 1296. His descendants did exceptionally well and in 1426, a John Phelyps was described as a chalonnere, someone who sold bedding.

Colmore Row in the 1950s, one of several streets recalling the Colmore family, the most powerful in Tudor Birmingham and influential as Lench's Trustees. The building on the left, on the corner with Newhall Street, was later demolished and replaced by a tower block. The buses in the background are by St. Phillip's Churchyard.

Like the Shiltons, the family moved away from trade and into landholding and property, with William Phillips featuring prominently in the great 1553 Survey of Birmingham. He freely held a house in 'Dygbathe' with a croft, and two fish ponds, land and buildings in Park Street. This was supplemented by the rent of land and buildings in Molle (Moor) Street, New Street, High Street, Dale End, and elsewhere. One intriguing rental related to a pasture called Bennetts Hill, for which William paid one rose at the feast of the Nativity of St. John the Baptist.

His son, Ambrose, inherited the family lands and was later described as a gentleman living in Walsall. No longer having to work, he'd entered the gentry. By the early seventeenth century, the Phillipses owned most of the land and dwellings they'd once rented, as well as much of New Street and the Bull Ring. The last of the family's direct line was Robert Phillips of Newton Regis near Tamworth. It was his wife, Elizabeth, who gave Horse Close on Bennetts Hill for the building of St. Philip's Church. Consecrated in 1715, it's now Birmingham Cathedral, carrying the name of a family deeply connected to Birmingham and the Lench's Trust. After Robert Phillips, his property passed through marriage to Theodore William Inge of Thorpe Constantine, recalled in Inge Street and Thorp Street.

Looking along Phillips Street, named after the family of one of Lench's Trustees, to Moor Street. The old Market Hall is to the right and the Fish Market to the left. The street and buildings were swept away in the post-1945 redevelopment of the Bull Ring.

The remaining Trustees included men connected to Lenche's five close friends. Henry Shilton was Symond's brother-in-law and a relative of John Shilton; William Hawkes was the father of Lenche's servant Roger Hawkes; and John Swyft was a relation of Richard Swyft. They were joined by William Paynton, Lenche's servant; Henry Sygwyk, related to an executor of Lenche's will and the owner of the Bull Tavern in Chapel Street, afterwards Bull Street; Thomas Spurriar, a landholder; Edward Pepwell, one of a family long connected with that of Lenche in Duddeston; William Askryk, a newcomer to Birmingham who was a landholder and active in public affairs; and Thomas Wygstyd and Robert Goldson, about whom nothing is known.

Chapter 2

Challenges and Survival

The Trust's Declaration, 1540

William Lenche died in 1526, and probate of his will was granted on 26 June in the joint names of Cardinal Thomas Wolsey, Archbishop of York and Chancellor of England, and William Warham, Archbishop of Canterbury. Then the most powerful man in England after the king, Wolsey was soon to lose favour for his failure to have Henry VIII's marriage to Catherine of Aragon annulled by the Pope. It seems that 13 years later, Agnes Lenche died and the Deed of Enfeoffment should have come into effect. Instead, an effort was made to thwart it.

John Marsh was grandson of John Lenche, William's uncle, and saw himself as the heir to the property and as such its owner. Swiftly, he sought to make money from it. In April 1539, he sold 20 acres of pasture in Duddeston, other properties and all of what he termed, "my lands, tenements, and rents in Birmingham".

In commemoration of William Lench, a tanner,
whose mortal remains lie buried beneath this church.
By deed of gift, dated 11th March 1525
he created Lench's Trust,
provider of almshouses in Birmingham
through the succeeding centuries.
(This plaque installed 11th March 2011)

The plaque commemorating William Lenche in St. Martin's Church in the Bull Ring.

In response, the four living Trustees who were the close friends of Lenche made the first Declaration of the Trust on 29 March 1540. Probably led by William Symonds, the others were John Shilton, Richard Swyft, and John Hipkys – Roger Redhyll having died. They made it clear that after the deaths of William and Agnes and by right of the Deed of Enfeoffment, they and their heirs "should stand and be seized of the premises … to distribute in works of charity according to our discretion and ordering, where we shall see the greater want". Emphasising that they desired "by no means the said feoffment should be disused nor forgotten but rather that it may be held in everlasting remembrance", they made grants of rental property to various people. These brought into sight Lenche's remaining holdings in the Trust: two tenements and land in Moor Street; a barn and a croft near to the Pinfold, where stray animals were kept in a pen and hence Pinfold Street; the Callowfields in Bordesley; and Hawke's Croft, pasture in part of what became the Gun Quarter and later the Trust's St. Mary's Estate.

The Declaration then listed other Trustees, including William Colmore the elder, the only other survivor of the original 19. Two others did have close connections with them. They were Roger Hawkes, a servant of Lench, who was probably the son of William Hawkes, and John King, a relative of William King. A fuller producing cloth from sheep's wool, John King had a fulling mill in

Smallbrook Queensway in early 1962, recalling the Smalbrokes, several of whom served as Trustees of Lench's. On the left is Ringway House designed by James Roberts, who also designed the Rotunda, and, on the right, the Albany Hotel is nearing completion.

Edgbaston and a dying house. The inventory of goods and chattels in his will of 1556 amounted to a considerable sum of £90.

One of that will's witnesses was Richard Smalbroke, another new Trustee who'd soon gain the prestigious and powerful office of High Bailiff, ensuring the legality of weights and measures in the town's markets. Recalled in Smallbrook Queensway, one of his sons was responsible for building Blakesley Hall, amongst Birmingham's oldest and most historically significant buildings and now a museum. As for Richard himself, he owned shops which he leased out and held property in Birmingham, Yardley, West Bromwich, and Bordesley, including the Ravenhurst Estate at Camp Hill that's remembered in Ravenhurst Street. After his direct line died out, his lands went through marriage to the Vyse family, hence Vyse Street in the Jewellery Quarter.

Smalbroke was also active in the wills of two other new Trustees, both of whom were wealthy tanners. The first was Henry Foxall, the son of Roger Foxall, a supervisor of Lenche's will; and the second was Thomas Marshall, whose goods were valued at a little over £130 after his death. He also bequeathed almost £60 in gold, silver, and money, whilst his will indicated that he'd lived in style in Park Street.

Two other newcomers to the Trust joined Smalbroke as amongst the most influential men in Birmingham: Humphrey Colchester was Master of the Guild of Holy Cross, and Robert Vernon was Birmingham's Low Bailiff, an officer of the Leet. In effect, this was the common assembly and court of justice of the township with Vernon summoning its juries and charging stallholders at the local fairs. The final new Trustees were Thomas Cowper, a prosperous scythesmith; landholders William Bogie and John Willeys; and John Vesey. Like Lench, Vesey was a grazier.

Indeed, he was one of the foremost locally, having numerous sheep folds, meadows, fields, and barns. Classed as a yeoman because he also held a small landed estate, he was below the rank of a gentleman but well above the generality of the population.

After their naming, the Trustees stated their intent to apply and distribute all income and profits arising from the lands and tenements in the Trust, setting out how they'd do that. Chosen annually with the assent of the majority, two of the feoffees would receive the money and use it to repair the ruined ways and bridges in and about Birmingham where there was need. In default of this, the rents and profits would be bestowed upon the poor living in the town where there was the greatest want, or else given over to other godly uses. At the end of each year, the assigned pair of feoffees would give a reasonable account of their distribution and non-distribution to their fellows in the chapel of St. Katherine in St. Martin's. Any funds not spent would be delivered to the other Trustees. After seven of the Trustees died, the survivors would enfeoff certain of the worthiest men of Birmingham.

Omnibus Xp̄i ffidelib̄ȝ ad quos hoc presens scrip̄t indentat̄ pueñit Wiłłs Symondys geños⁹ Joñes Shilton Riču̇s Swyfte et Joñes hipkys salt̄m in dño sempit̄nam. Cu̇m Wiłłm⁹ lenche deffunct̄ dederat et concesserat nobis p̄ffat̄ Wiłło Joñi Riĉo Joñi hipk̄c ac cuidā Roḡȷo Redhill deffunct̄ oĩa et singula suas t̄ras tenement̄ prat̄ pasĉ et pastur̄ reddit̄ reůĉ et serviĉ cu̇ oĩbȝ et singulis eoȝ ptinẽs iacent̄ et existent̄ in viłł et campis de Birmynghm̄ Dudston Bordisley p̄ua Bromewich et Saltley in Com̄ Warwiĉ ñend et tenend nobis et here-dibȝ nr̄is Cumqȝ nobis p̄ffat̄ ffeoffat̄ de p̄miss̄ racioĉ dict̄ feof-fament̄ existentibȝ seisit̄ ad opus et vsu̇ dict̄ Wiłłmi Lenche et hered̄ suorũ Dict̄ wiłłs lenche p̄ vltimā voluntat̄ suā int̄ʳ cet̄ʳa ordinauit et voluit q̄d nos de p̄miss̄ starem̄ʳ et existerem̄ʳ seisit̄ ad opus et vsu̇ dict̄ Wiłłi Lenche et cuidam Agnet̄ Lenche vxor̄ȷ ei⁹ p̄ t̄mïo vite eorũ vell alt̄ʳï⁹ eoȝ diuci⁹ vivent̄ et post eoȝ decessũ ad opus et vsu̇ nr̄oȝ p̄fat̄ Wiłłi Joñis Riĉi et Joñis Hypk̄c et hered̄ nroȝ ad distribuend in opa charita-tiua scd̄m discreciõem et ordinaciõem nr̄as p̄ut nobis maxime oportunũ et necessariũ visum fuerit. Nos p̄fat̄ feoffatores vsus p̄dict̄ haud imẽmores feoffamentũqȝ p̄dict̄ insolesser̄ minime volent̄ nec oblivioni tradi sed vt eternā mage conse-

The first page of the First Declaration of the Trust in 1540, written in Latin.

Empowered by the wealth and influence of 16 of the town's most significant citizens, the Trustees acted vigorously to regain control of their properties taken and sold by Lenche's second cousin, Marsh. In October 1540, Jasper Smythe, alias Hoysen, released all his claims to various lands, tenements, rents, and services in Birmingham and elsewhere to the Trustees. Much more of Lenche's Estate was bought from Marsh by Edward Pye, a gentleman of Ward End, then on the outskirts of Birmingham. On 2 April 1541, an Indenture of Arbitration settled all variance, strife, and debate arising from divers ambiguities and doubts concerning Marsh's heirship and the feoffment, with Pye receiving £20 in full satisfaction of all claims. Six months later, he received a further £10 for his final release of all claims and deeds of Lenche's lands.

More difficulty was had in pursuing claims against Thomas Holte, who'd bought substantial lands, tenements, rents, reversions, and services from Marsh's daughter, Margaret. A big landowner owning the manors of Nechells, Duddeston, and Aston, Holte was a successful and unscrupulous lawyer benefitting from Henry VIII's dissolution of the monasteries.

Failing in his attempts to get the Pope to annul his marriage to Katherine of Aragon, Henry VIII broke with papal authority and in 1534, the Act of Supremacy made him Supreme Head of the Church in England. This was quickly followed by two acts of suppression disbanding Roman Catholic monasteries, priories, convents, and friaries, and allowing the king to seize their wealth and dispose of their assets. Looking for a swift return on his new estates, he sold them at competitive prices, giving his henchmen an unparalleled opportunity to increase their holdings, status, and influence.

Amongst those taking advantage was Holte, probably one of the Visiting Commissioners appointed by the king to oversee the dissolution regionally. On the same day as Pye's final release in favour of the Trustees, 6 April 1541, Holte did the same. The strength of the Trustees was underscored by their determination to challenge such a formidable opponent, yet it was only a partial victory because Lenche's lands in Aston and Duddeston were not included. They were lost, in all likelihood, to Holte.

Loveday Croft and Expansion

Under Henry's son, Edward VI, a final attack was made on Catholic religious bodies. In 1547, all religious guilds were dissolved with their property confiscated by the crown and sold on. In Deritend, the Guild of St. John disappeared. So too did Birmingham's Guild of the Holy Cross, although Richard Smalbroke and others petitioned successfully for some of the funds raised from the sale of its estates and other property to be restored for educational purposes. This led to the 1552 charter founding the King Edward VI School, which was supported by grants of land, including the site of the Guild House. The 20 Governors of the new school almost replicated Lench's existing Trustees. In addition to Smalbroke others were Symonds, Shilton, Swyft, Colmore the elder, Marshall, Foxall, Vesey, Bogie, King, Cowper, and Willeys. Three more governors were closely connected to the Trust: Paynton; William Colmore the younger; and Ascrick, an original Trustee.

Lench's Trust was fortunate not to be dissolved as its provisions were practically the same as those granted to the Guild of the Holy Cross in 1392. In his pioneering work on English Guilds, Joshua Toulmin Smith believed that even though the Trust didn't maintain a priest, it escaped for two reasons. Firstly, it was called a trust and not a guild and secondly, it was established by enfeoffment and not by a licence in mortmain, a document issued by the Crown for the alienation or conveyance of lands to a monastery or other corporation.

Having survived, Lench's gained from a donation of William Colmore the elder. In his will of 1566, he gave it an annuity or yearly rent charge of 10 shillings from a house with outbuildings and some land in Corn Cheaping, close to the top of Moor Street and now part of the Bull Ring. Another more substantial addition was more puzzling in how it came about. This was the four acres of Loveday's Croft, later part of the St. Mary's Estate and remembered in Loveday Street. In his *Canterbury Tales*, Chaucer stated that the friar "in lovedays there could he much help", indicating that on such occasions he would facilitate the amicable settling of disputes in certain spots. According to tradition, Loveday Croft was so named because it was given over by John Cowper for the making of lovedays amongst Birmingham men.

This belief was strengthened by entries in the Trust's minute books. Kept from 1771, they recorded payments from Loveday Croft's rents of 2 shillings 6 pence a time or for "composing a difference", "temporising a difference", "an arbitration", "making up a lawsuit", and "making peace". Joseph Hill, a dedicated researcher into Birmingham's past, believed that the payments actually didn't begin until many years after Lench's was founded. In support, he noted that the earliest relevant deed for Loveday Croft from 1564 indicated it was leased to William Cowper, scythesmith, for a payment of £5 "towards the repairing and amending of the Stone Bridge, called Rea Bridge, in Birmingham … in ruin and decay". Formerly looked after by the Guild of the Holy Cross, its condition had deteriorated badly since its dissolution.

The 1524-25 Lay Subsidy recorded a John Cowper (Cooper) as amongst the wealthiest men in Birmingham and it may be it was he who put Loveday Croft in trust. Although no documentary evidence exists, the 1564 document did name three Trustees. They were Thomas Cowper, Richard Smalbroke, and John Vesey, all of whom were also feoffees of Lench's. By 1584, only Vesey survived in both trusts and that year, he joined with William Bothe, a yeoman, in bringing Loveday Croft into Lench's – although only Vesey is commemorated in a street name. This was achieved by conveyance of the properties to a pair of intermediate Trustees, William Severne, tanner, and William Woodwall, Master of the Free School (King Edward VI). Two years later, they conveyed Lenche's lands to Vesey, Bothe, and 12 other Trustees. Amongst them were the sons or close relatives of previous feoffees: John Shilton, mercer; William King, ironmonger; William Colmore the younger and his cousin, Ambrose the younger, both mercers; and Thomas Smalbroke, yeoman.

The new names included John Ward the elder, a wealthy yeoman owning land and buildings in Birmingham, Aston, Little Bromwich, Castle Bromwich, and Bordesley; and his cousin, John Ward, a prosperous baker whose father set up a trust that would become part of Lench's. Edward Smith was connected to them through his wife, Joan. She was a daughter of William Colmore the elder and after his death, her widowed mother (also Joan) married John Ward the elder. The Trustees' numbers were made up with other well-to-do men: Robert Rastell, draper; Thomas Smith, wine merchant; Thomas Selman, whose goods and

Built upon from the late 1700s, Loveday Croft was transformed into Loveday Street amid Birmingham's Gun Quarter as shown by the St. Mary's Works of the renowned gunmaker, W. W. Greener.

chattels were worth £55 when he died in 1603; and Robert Whittall, ironmonger, one of whose descendants bought the Crossfields Estate close to Loveday Croft and is brought to mind by Whittall Street by the Children's Hospital.

No documents relating specifically to the Trust survived between 1586 and 1613 when the two remaining Trustees, Whittall and Ambrose Colmore, made 12 new feoffees and renewed the settlement of Lenche's lands. Amongst them were familiar names: three more of the Colmore family, two Smalbrokes, and another Smith and Whittall. They were joined by Roger Pemberton, a rich goldsmith whose descendants became Quakers and who, through marriage, brought the banking Lloyds to Birmingham from Wales. The final four Trustees were Edward Lea, a woollen draper from a well-established family, and three tanners: Richard White the younger, John Carter, and John Foxall, a relative of an earlier Trustee.

Chapter 3

Seventeenth-Century Consolidation

Commission, Inquisition, and Decree, 1628

Towards the end of Elizabeth I's reign, the state began taking a keen interest in charities and in 1601 the Charitable Uses Act was passed. It aimed "to redress the misemployment of lands, goods and stocks of money heretofore given to charitable uses" and to encourage private donations to causes considered beneficial to society. Towards these ends, the Act's introductory preamble outlined a list of purposes regarded as legitimate, thus laying the foundations for modern definitions of charitable intentions. This list included purposes pertinent to Lench's: the relief of aged, impotent, and poor people and the repair of bridges.

It was under this Act, making charities more accountable legally, that the Trustees faced a severe problem when, on 27 July 1627, "A Commission of Charitable Uses for the County of Warwick" was issued. Eighteen high-status men were given full power and authority as Commissioners to make inquiries into charitable holdings of all kinds in Warwickshire. They included Sir Thomas Holte, the grandson of Thomas Holte who'd probably profited by gaining Lenche's estates in Aston and Duddeston, and Sir John Shilton, solicitor general to Charles I and grandson of Lenche's close friend and Trustee, John Shilton. However, as a minimum of four Commissioners were required to investigate each charity, neither were involved in the Inquisition of Lench's Trust, which also involved 17 lawful Jurors. Men from amongst the county's leading families, swore upon oath as to its findings.

Written on three skins of parchment, the Inquisition was taken on 25 March 1628 before six Commissioners and 17 Jurors in Birmingham. It's not known where, although the only suitable building would have been the old Guild Hall which had become King Edward VI School. The document itself is a long one, detailing Lench's history and examining in detail all relevant deeds and wills. Some misemployment was found. As the surviving feoffees, in 1573, Vesey and Richard Smalbroke leased a farm to the latter's son for 99 years at a rent that was lower than the true value of the properties. Eleven years later, William Colmore the younger benefited from a lease of two tenements and part of a croft in Moor Street granted by Vesey – then the only remaining Trustee. Colmore would join him two years later and, of course, his father was an original feoffee. Other examples of favouritism followed. In 1613, a barn and croft were rented to a pair of Smalbrokes to farm for 21 years at the end of the existing beneficial lease. A year later, in February 1614, Robert Whittall and Ambrose Colmore were the two surviving Trustees and they leased Loveday Croft to Colmore's son on the same terms. A few months afterwards, the favour was returned when Hawkes Croft was leased to Edward Whittall, who would become a Trustee in October.

Nurses from the General Hospital in 1939 at the outbreak of the Second World War in Whittall Street. Named after a family prominent as Trustees in Lench's, the street name is on the right of the hospital wall in the background.

Having made their Inquisition, the Commissioners were empowered to set down decrees ensuring that all lands, annuities, gifts, goods, chattels, rents, properties, money, and stocks of money would be duly and faithfully employed according to the wishes of the founders and donors. This they did. The decree wasn't dated but it must have been issued before 5 May 1628 when it was delivered to the Court along with the Inquisition.

The decree ordered that the rents and profits from Lench's lands and Loveday Croft would forever be employed to the same uses as declared in 1540:

> … for repairing the ways and bridges ruinous or in decay, or hereafter to be ruinous or in decay, in and about the aforesaid town of Birmingham, where need shall be; and for default of such use, that the same shall be distributed to and amongst the poor dwelling within said Town of Birmingham, where most need shall be, according to the discretion, order, and disposition of the feoffees of the said lands for the time being, or of the greater part of them; or to other godly uses.

It's apparent that the Trustees had neglected their chief undertaking to repair ruinous ways and bridges as the Commissioners found that Deritend Bridge was in great decay. They ordered it to be repaired with all convenient speed, allowing the Trustees to sell off timber from their lands to raise money for the work. The problems with leases were addressed as firmly. Having property worth just over £21 annually in all outcomings, it was declared that the Trust's charitable uses could not in any part be defrauded, nor its rents and profits misemployed. Long leases and those in reversion were dismissed as unfitting and those recorded in the Inquisition were decreed void in law and ordered to be surrendered. New leases, with clauses for non-payment, were to last no more than 21 years and were to be at the annual values stated in the Inquisition. All deeds and writings of the Trust had to be kept in a chest at St. Martin's Church or another convenient place and it was to be secured with at least three locks, each key kept by a separate Trustee.

Henceforth, when seven feoffees were left alive they were to appoint "the most honest and sufficient inhabitants" of Birmingham to make a total of at least 14. Two of them should be chosen annually as Bailiffs to gather and distribute the Trusts' rents and profits. Each year on the Tuesday afternoon of Easter week and upon the tolling of a bell, they were to account for their dealings at a meeting of the Trustees and other inhabitants. Any money remaining was to be handed over to the two bailiffs replacing them.

The Writ for the Execution of the Decree was issued on 9 October 1628 and following on from the Inquisition document, the 'e' was dropped from William Lenche's name. Henceforth his Trust was to be Lench's and for the next 250 years, it was administered in accordance with that Decree. On 4 April 1629, Lench's lands were vested in 19 Trustees. Nine of them carried on from those appointed 16 years before.

Richard Smalbroke and Edward Colmore now deemed themselves gentlemen whilst their relatives Thomas Smalbroke and Ambrose Colmore still

CAROLUS Dei gr̄a Angl Scotie ffranc̄ ꝥ Hib̄n Rex fidei defensor tc̄. Ricardo Smalbroke Edwardo Colmore ꝥ Thome Smalbroke ac om̄ibӡ aliis quibuscunꝙ, quoӡ int̄est aut int̄esse pot̄it saltm. Cumque ex cōi consilio regni nr̄i Angl ad Dei gl̄iam ꝥ ppl̄i nr̄i cōmodum puisa sunt ꝥ ordinata ea nos p regia authoritate nr̄a debite execuc̄oi mandari teneam͛ Ac nup ex c̄tificac̄oe Rog̃li Burgoyne, armig̃li, Thome Peake armig̃li, Ric̄i Weston, armig̃li, Rad̄i Bowne, gen̄osi, Rolandi ffrith, gen̄osi, ꝥ Henr̄ Cookꞓ, gen̄osi, Cōmissionar̄ nr̄oӡ (int̄ alios) virtute Cōmissionis nr̄e sub magno sigillo nr̄o Angl eis in hac parte direc̄t ꝥ in Cancellar̄ nr̄am vnacum quadam Inquisic̄oe retornat̄ ꝥ miss̄ ac in filaciis ejusdem Cancellar̄ nr̄e de recordo residñ dat͛ not̄ intelligi, qd̄ p̄v̄fati Cōmissionar̄, nr̄i virtute dc̄e Cōmissionis nr̄e iuxta formam cuiusdam Actus in Parliamento Dñe Elizabeth nup Regine Angl anno regni sui quadragesimo l̄cio tent̄ edit̄ ꝥ pv̄is̄ fc̄a prius p p̄riam dc̄a Inquisic̄oe hitisꝙ, debita testiū exaīac̄oe ꝥ delib̄ac̄oe matura ordinac̄oes quasdam siue decret̄ in scriptis de ꝥ conc̄ñeñ (int̄ alia) quoddam ffeoffamentum quoӡdam terr̄ ꝥ teñ vocat̄ Lenches landꞓ in Birmingham in com̄ nr̄o Warr̄ ac de quadam añuitate siue annuali reddit̄ on̄is decem solid̄ exeuñ de vno Burgagio siue mesuagio cum ptiñ in Birmingham p̄v̄dic̄t scituat̄ in le Corne Chippingꞓ ib̄m ac ad supiorem angulum vici ib̄m vocat̄ Moorestreete al̄s Molestreite Ac de vno teñ cum ptiñ scituat̄ iaceñ ꝥ existeñ in Birmingham p̄v̄dic̄t in quodam vico ib̄m vocat̄ Mercers streete modo in tenur̄ cuiusdam Will̄i Halfepeny Ac de vno Crofto siue parcell̄ terr̄ cum ptin vocat̄ Woodcockes Crofte, iaceñ infra ffeodum de Dudstone in com̄ p̄v̄dc̄o Ac de vna clausura siue parcella terr̄ in Birmingham p̄v̄dic̄t vocat̄ Loveday Crofte vni vel pluribӡ talibӡ psonis ville de Birmingham pdic̄t ea intenc̄oe

The first page of the Writ for the Execution of the Decree, 9 October 1628.

traded as mercers. Richard White remained a tanner. Edward Lea continued as a woollen draper and Edward Whittall gave himself as a yeoman. The final two were now based in London: formerly a tanner, John Carter called himself a yeoman, whilst Thomas Smith still plied his trade as a vintner.

They were joined by ten new men ordered by the Commissioners, including seven connected to existing or previous Trustees: William Colmore and Robert Shilton, gentlemen; Robert Smalbroke, mercer; Thomas Pemberton, goldsmith; Ambrose Foxall, tanner; and John Carter the younger, tanner. To them were added Humprey Vaughton, a butcher brought to mind in Vaughton Street, Highgate; John Jennens, an ironmonger whose family became fabulously wealthy and who's recalled in Jennens Row; and John Billingsley, tanner. The Commissioners showed noticeable care not only in appointing the "most honest and sufficient inhabitants of Birmingham" but also in ensuring they included representatives of the most important trades in the town as well as those rising into the gentry.

Amalgamations 1628 and 1668: Crofts, Doles, and Bell Ropes

In their Inquisition, the Commissioners confirmed Loveday Croft as belonging to Lench's Trust along with William Colmore the elder's bequest of an annual rent of 10 shillings from the building in Corn Cheaping. Their Decree also included another gift connected to him, that of Woodcock's Croft, now the educational quarter around Woodcock Street in the city centre. Originally the land was left in trust by Reverend John Shingler, whose family were involved with the Holtes. There's no record of when he enfeoffed it, however as he was noted in a document from 1436 it must have been well before the end of the fifteenth century. If so, this would make it the oldest known Birmingham charity. In 1517, his Trustees conveyed it to four others, all of whom would become Trustees of Lench's. The last of these was William Colmore the elder, and in 1554, he enfeoffed 14 others. Their declaration and distribution of rents copied Lench's, unsurprisingly as they shared seven trustees.

One other amalgamation was ordered by the Commissioners, the Trust of William Wrixham. Formerly parson of St. Martin's, in 1578 he bequeathed his house in Mercer Street (Spiceal Street in the Bull Ring) to six Trustees with the familiar names of Shilton, Colmore, Vesey, Smalbroke, Smith, and Rastell. Wrixham willed that each year on Good Friday and according to their discretion, they should distribute the rents and profits from his building to the poor of Birmingham where there was the greatest need. In addition, he left 40 shillings to be distributed to the poor on his burial day; the same sum for similar purposes for the next two years on Christmas Day and Good Friday; 10 shillings for the repair of Salford Bridge over the River Tame, close to where the traffic on Spaghetti Junction now roars; and 10 shillings for the poor of Aston along with four pairs of sheets one month after his decease.

These two amalgamations strengthened Lench's Trust and provided the precedent for the addition of other smaller charities in 1668 as indicated by an indenture from a few years later. The first merger was related to the Ward family. Established in Little Bromwich from the end of the thirteenth century, they were major landowners locally and gave their name to Ward End. By a deed of 1573, John Ward granted his house and land at Marston Culey (Marston Green) to John Vesey and others, two of whom would receive the rents and distribute them twice a year to the poor and needy of Birmingham. Called John Ward's Dole, this income remained within the Trust until the property was sold in 1856.

Woodcock Street in the 1950s shortly before these back-to-back houses were cleared. They were built on Woodcock Croft.

Looking down Spiceal Street in the early 1950s before the redevelopment of the Bull Ring. Originally called Mercer Street, it was the site of the house bequeathed by William Wrixham to a trust which became part of Lench's.

A second addition resulted from John Shilton, one of the leading figures amongst the original feoffees of Lench's, leaving 10 shillings a year to the poor of Birmingham forever. By the mid-1600s, this and various other monies given for charitable purposes locally were in the hands of one group of Trustees. These other gifts appear to have derived from benefactions publicised on tablets in St. Martin's Church. In 1612, Edward Smith gave £20, the benefit of which was to be distributed annually to the poor. A generation later, Barnaby Smith left the same amount to be lent to poor tradesmen for two or three years at the discretion of the churchwardens; and in 1642, his wife, Catherine, gave another £20 for the poor, again at the discretion of the churchwardens. Then in 1651, John Jennings left 50 shillings a year forever for making coats for poor aged people born and living in Birmingham as well as 20 shillings to be handed to the poor of the town annually.

In 1654 and in 'satisfaction' for Shilton's sum and the payment of £86 10 shillings, presumably from the other monies, his great grandson granted 22 feoffees a house in Moor Street adjoining Lench's. It came with an acre of land and appendages, namely a croft of two acres in the Summer Lane area, later the Brass Street Estate. In effect, this grant was a purchase probably engineered by Thomas Peake. One of the feoffees, he was a cousin of Shilton's descendant and an influential man who was one of the six Commissioners signing the 1628 Decree. Another powerful feoffee was Robert Turton, who was also a Lench's Trustee. Originally a Birmingham draper, he became a captain in the Parliamentary Army in the English Civil War. As the agreement was signed during the Protectorate, the period when Oliver Cromwell in effect ruled England following the defeat of the Royalists, Turton's involvement must have carried much weight.

Bell Rope Croft was also conveyed to Lench's in 1668. Narrow and deep and facing onto the modern Broad Street, it was so called because all its rents and profits were paid to the churchwardens of St. Martin's to buy its bell ropes. Then still a mediaeval structure, the church had three bells, a clock, and a chime in its tower. The croft's rent was 8 shillings, rising to £8 in the 1820s. In 1880, the Trustees requested that the Charity Commissioners found a separate charity for the property. This they did and Bell Rope Croft continues, though there is no longer a croft. It was remembered in St. Martin's Row, which disappeared with the redevelopment of the area for Brindley Place and the ICC. The 1668 deed is the earliest for this land, as it was for the Digbeth almshouses, although they were first mentioned in 1639 in the Trust's accounts.

The final gain by Lench's in 1668 arose from a donation made by Richard Kilcuppe. In his will of 1611, he gifted two Trustees with a house and meadow in Bordesley. Later the Trust's Sparkbrook Estate, this was almost five acres fronting the modern Stratford Road, Farm Road, and Grantham Road. The Trustees were directed to convey the land to "20 discreet inhabitants in Birmingham for charitable uses to be for ever done and continued". The next year, they declared that 13 shillings 4 pence should be paid annually to the churchwardens of St. Martin's towards its repair with the remainder of the income to be bestowed for the relief of the town's poor, aged, and impotent. Kilcuppe was a generous man and set up another charity specifically for Bordesley, which included not only the modern district but also Small Heath and much of Bordesley Green and Sparkbrook. That Trust continues separately.

The narrow St. Martin's Place, the former Bell Rope Croft, is on the right. On the left is the Unitarian Church of the Messiah spanning the Birmingham Canal and in the background is St. Peter's Catholic Church. They were demolished as part of the ICC/Brindley Place developments in the late twentieth century.

Chapter 4

Charitable Trustees

Exactly why and how the 1668 amalgamations happened isn't known. However, Lench's was obviously the most important charity in Birmingham and its Trustees were amongst the most important men in the town, some of whom were involved in the merged good causes.

Notably, this process happened the year after a deed vested Lench's lands in 23 Trustees. They included Abraham Colmore. At least one of his family, and sometimes two or three, had been appointed at each vesting of the Deed since 1525. Two other Trustees, Samuel and Thomas Smalbroke, had unbroken links back to 1540. Of the rest appointed in 1667, only the cutlers Ambrose and John Foxall had a close connection with the Trust's beginnings. Becoming wealthy, most of the descendants of the original feoffees moved away from Birmingham, a town that was expanding rapidly in the late seventeenth century and pulling in many newcomers from the surrounding counties. They included Henry Fentham, a tanner, and his brother, George, a mercer.

Raised in Hampton in Arden as the sons of a churchwarden, the Fenthams did well, with George buying land in Erdington. Having no children, after his death in 1698, he left the income from certain properties in two trusts: one for his home village and another for Birmingham, which originally received £20 a year. This sum was split in half: to pay for the relief of the poor of the town and to instruct poor boys and girls "to know their letters, spell, and read English". All those benefiting had to live within 200 yards of the Bull Ring. Writing a century later, William Hutton, Birmingham's first historian, explained that Fentham was motivated because he'd "spent a life in Birmingham, knew well her inhabitants, and like some others, had found honour as well as riches among them. He knew also, he could with safety deposit his property in their hands and was determined it should never go out". The George Fentham Birmingham Charity and the George Fentham Trust in Hampton in Arden continue to do excellent work.

Two of their first Trustees were also represented on Lench's. They were Ambrose Foxall, a cutler, and George Jackson, a prosperous woollen draper and cousin of Fentham. Belonging to a family long established in Birmingham, Jackson was a most generous man, leaving property in Deritend in trust, with the income used to place poor Birmingham boys as apprentices. Today, George

The Prospect of Birmingham *in 1656 in William Dugdale's* The Antiquities of Warwickshire *is the first known pictorial representation of the town. St. Martin's Church is prominent on the left and to the right Digbeth goes downhill to the Valley of the Rea. Across the river, the large building is St. John's Church, the chapel noted by Leland in 1538. This view was taken from Ravenhurst, the wooded hill of ravens, recalled in Ravenhurst Street, Camp Hill. Then it was the name of an estate owned by the Smalbroke family, members of which were influential Trustees until the later seventeenth century.*

Jackson's Educational Foundation annually makes awards to students in the final year at "Birmingham City University (Department of the Arts, Design & Media) to enable them to further their studies by travelling, usually for research purposes".

Marked changes in the makeup of Lench's Trustees became noticeable by 1691 when the remaining seven Trustees were supplemented with 16 new members. For the first time, there was no Colmore. Nor was there a Smalbroke. The only ones left connected to the start of the Trust were the cutlers Foxall and his son, John, the last of his line associated with the Trust. The older man had been a tanner like his forebears and Lenche, but with that trade declining locally, he'd moved into Birmingham's burgeoning metal trades making cutlery. Indeed, there was no tanner amongst the new Trustees, although there were four ironmongers and two mercers carrying on the involvement of those trades since 1525. Contrastingly, apart from three gentlemen, the others were drawn from a more diverse background with two dyers and a bridle cutter, sadler, chandler, and maltster.

The shifting composition of the Trustees accelerated with the rapid growth of Birmingham and the transformation of its economy. In 1732, William Westley declared that by the art and industry of its inhabitants, the town had "for some years past been rendered famous all over the World, for the choice and invention of all sorts of Wares and Curiosities, in Iron, Steel, Brass &c: admired as well for their cheapness as for their peculiar beauty of Workmanship". On its way to becoming the city of 1,000 trades, Birmingham was no longer a centre of tanning but of the making of guns, coins, buckles, buttons, silver plate, japanned ware, and much more.

Interestingly, though, the leading manufacturers in these trades didn't become involved with the Trust. Neither Matthew Boulton of the acclaimed Lunar Society nor James Watt of steam engine fame joined. Nor did John Taylor the Birmingham button king, Sampson Lloyd the co-founder of Lloyds Bank, Samuel Galton senior the large scale gunmaker, and John Baskerville, the japanner and celebrated printer.

Instead, by 1742, the Trustees were mostly a mix of men involved in the metal trades and providing services. There were six ironmongers, three cutlers, and a shear maker as well as three bakers, two maltsters, a thread maker, chandler, linen draper, apothecary, and a barber/peruke maker. Their number was made up by one gentleman. None were amongst 'the princes of industry' launching Birmingham onto the global market as a pre-eminent manufacturing town.

Westley's East Prospect of Birmingham, 1731. *On the bottom left is St. John's Chapell, Deritend and just above it is Deritend Bridge, the repairs for which were the responsibility of Lench's. The spire is that of St. Martin's in the Bull Ring and on the hill is the recently built St. Philip's, now Birmingham's Cathedral. The land around the small built-up area was gardens or fields.*

Chapter 5

A Unitarian Takeover?

Eighteenth-Century Unitarian Influence

By the mid-eighteenth century, Lench's was no longer overseen by the most important and wealthy men in Birmingham, although one notable manufacturing family was active as Trustees. John Webster, an ironmonger at Penns Mills, was appointed in 1721, the year after he founded Webster and Horsfall. Later renowned for inventing the first transatlantic cable wire which revolutionised global communication, the company remains a world-class producer of high-quality, speciality wires in Hay Mills. In 1755, Webster was followed by his son, Joseph, a wire drawer who developed crucible steel as a means of producing steel wire, and in 1777, he was joined by his son, Joseph the younger. They were members of the Church of England but related to a leading Unitarian family in Birmingham and it was the appointment of Unitarians which signalled the revival of the bond between the Trust and some of Birmingham's most notable men.

As members of a Christian sect dissenting from the Church of England established by law as the national church, like other Non-Conformists, Unitarians were discriminated against legally. Disallowed from becoming MPs, holding public office, entering the civil service, and gaining university degrees, they still had to pay local taxes to the Anglican Church and be married by its ministers. But as they weren't excluded from business, they threw their energies into their work and in Birmingham many became highly successful owners of manufacturing concerns.

Small in numbers, they were economically powerful but deeply affected by their religious beliefs, many became involved in public affairs. Active in campaigns against religious discrimination and for a more liberal society, they sought ways to help those less fortunate than themselves. Involvement with Lench's Trust was a means to that end.

The Unitarian influence began unobtrusively soon after the sect's emergence in Birmingham with the appointment of two prominent members out of 22 Trustees in 1667. The first was George Jackson, founder of the charities named after him and a trustee of Kilcuppe's Gift. As such it's likely that he had a hand in its merger with Lench's. In 1689, Jackson was also one of 11 men who paid for the building of the first Unitarian Chapel in Birmingham, the Old Meeting in Dudley Street just off the Bull Ring. Another was John Baker, the second Unitarian joining the Trust. A chandler, dealer in household items, he was engaged in various aspects of the town's affairs. In 1691, after Jackson's death, Baker was joined on Lench's by John Gisborne, a dyer and mercer and a trustee of Jackson's Charity. So too was William Guest, a maltster and another newcomer to Lench's that year. These Unitarians remained a small minority amongst the Trustees, but their numbers grew noticeably in the succeeding years.

The renewal of the Deed and vesting of the Trustees in 1721, the first of the eighteenth century, was groundbreaking in that two of the seven witnesses were women. One was Sarah Brooks, about whom nothing is known, and the other was Mary Baker, perhaps the wife or daughter of John Baker. He, Guest, and Gisborne were joined as Trustees by two fellow Unitarians, William Haddock, a chandler, and Jonathan Grier, a linen draper. Both were successful in business, eventually retiring and becoming gentlemen, and both served the Trust faithfully for 50 years. They were last named in 1770, by which date there were 11 Unitarians out of 21 trustees.

They included Thomas Colmore, a merchant descended from a junior line of the original feoffee William Colmore the elder. Another was James Jackson, a jeweller, warden at the Old Meeting, and Low Bailiff of Birmingham. This was one of the two most important positions in the town. Until it was incorporated in 1838, Birmingham had no council to run its affairs. Instead, there were three main authorities: justices charged with keeping the peace and punishing crime; parish officers who relieved the poor, supervised the repair of roads, and paid the constables to keep the peace; and the Leet, the most ancient of the three. Exercising authority through a jury at its annual meeting, the Leet was responsible for markets, nuisances

The Old Meeting in Dudley Street, the first Unitarian place of worship in Birmingham. (Library of Birmingham).

and other matters, either belonging to the lord of the manor or interfering with his rights. Its daily functions were charged to several officers, the most powerful of whom were the high bailiff, who ensured the legality of weights and measures in the markets, and the low bailiff, who summoned juries to the Leet. From 1732, it became customary for the high bailiff to be a member of the Church of England and the low bailiff to be a Unitarian.

The son of a previous low bailiff, Michael Lakin the elder was also amongst the new Unitarian Trustees in 1770. Living in Moor Street, he was a glazer and plumber prominent in the building trade. One the founders of the Protestant Dissenting School, he served the Trust until his death in 1789 when it was said of him that "his private worth and public zeal were great". Kindly and indefatigably attentive to the affairs of the General Hospital, his loss to that charity would be very sensibly met. (*Aris's Birmingham Gazette*, 25 May 1789).

With the renewal of the deeds in 1777, Unitarians reinforced their presence with 15 out of the 21 trustees. In addition to James Jackson, they included leading figures from the congregation: Thomas Lawrence, a hatter; Benjamin May, a plater; Joseph Tyndall, a merchant; Robert Mason, a gentleman; and Abel Humphrys, formerly a draper and now a gentleman. Humphreys was another who'd been low bailiff, a position that would be held by one more new Unitarian Trustee, Samuel Pemberton the younger, a jeweller and later a guardian of the Assay Office. Mentioned as goldsmiths as far back as the later sixteenth century, some of the Pembertons were ironmongers and money lenders, and with their riches from business they became significant landowners locally.

The Unitarian majority on the Trust quickly instituted quarterly meetings to supplement the annual event at St. Martin's. With no offices, they decided to hold them at the Leicester Arms. A tavern and coffee house just off the Bull Ring, it was run by the Unitarian John Freeth, who witnessed several of the Trust's deeds of renewal and whose premises were used for Unitarian vestry meetings. Dubbed 'Freeth the poet' because of his output of ballads, he was a radical advocating religious tolerance and political reform. Drawing similar-minded people to his tavern, it became the venue for the Birmingham Book Club, which sought to spread knowledge rather than restrict it.

Most were Unitarians as were the '12 Apostles', Freeth and 11 of his friends who discussed often controversial ideas in a convivial setting. Powerful local conservatives who hated liberal thought called them the Jacobin Club. That was a dangerous title. The most famous political group in the French Revolution, the Jacobins were feared for their extreme violence and role in the 'Reign of Terror', when thousands of their opponents were executed.

Regarded as supporters of the French Revolution and as a danger to the established order, resentment against Unitarians was exacerbated by their wealth

John Wilkes. Richard Webster. Jeremiah Vaux.

James Murray. John Freeth.   John Collard. John Miles.   John Toy.   Joseph Fearon Joseph Blunt.

THE FREETH CIRCLE: FROM THE TONTINE PICTURE BY ECKSTEIN.

'Poet' Freeth's Circle from a painting by Johannes Eckstein. Freeth is sitting second from the left.

and high status in a town where most of the poor were Church of England. That resentment boiled into a dangerous anger which erupted into several days of violence in 1791. Church and king mobs went on the rampage. After burning down the Old Meeting and the more recent New Meeting, they sacked the houses of wealthy Unitarian families and forced their celebrated minister, the scientist and member of the Lunar Society, Joseph Priestley, to flee from Birmingham.

John Ryland, another new Trustee in 1777, was one of those who suffered. Hailing from Stratford-upon-Avon, he ran a wire drawing works and quickly made a lot of money, although he also benefited greatly from his marriage to Martha Ruston, a wealthy heiress. Ryland, though, was praised by Hutton as more than a successful manufacturer, for he was "a friend to the whole human race. He had done more public business than any other within my knowledge, and not only without reward, but without a fault". Those qualities meant little to the infuriated mob who stormed out of town to Ryland's mansion on Easy Hill. Now the site of Baskerville House facing Centenary Square, then it stood "in the midst of a luxuriant meadow," and was approached by a fine avenue of trees. It was gutted and set on fire. Several bodies were later found in its cellar, but fortunately the Rylands had fled.

Powerful Nineteenth-Century Unitarian Trustees

Ryland was a former low bailiff and his son, Samuel, also went on to hold that post. A Trustee from 1789, he married Samuel Pemberton's daughter, Anne, and having made his fortune from manufacturing and his mother, he followed the example of the Colmores and Shiltons in leaving industrial Birmingham to become a gentleman with a landed estate. This was at Barford Hill House in Sherbourne, near Stratford-upon-Avon. His daughter and heir, Louisa Anne, was a child but never forgot Birmingham. Never marrying, she became its most bounteous benefactor. Contributing thousands of pounds to church building and charities, in 1873 she gave the land for Cannon Hill Park, paying for it to be drained, laid out, and planted. She also presented Small Heath Park, and helped the Women's Hospital, the Birmingham and Midland Institute, and the School of Art in Edmund Street, now the Birmingham Institute of Art and Design and part of the University of Central England.

Various Rylands still involved in manufacturing continued as Trustees until 1848, when they were succeeded by Arthur Ryland, a solicitor and cousin of

Several generations of the wealthy Rylands were Trustees of Lench's. Owning much of Ladywood, they're recalled in Ryland Street and Ryland Road, on the right of this photo from the 1950s. The housing was back-to-back, with terraces at the back of those fronting the street.

Louisa Ann. His obituary in the *Birmingham Post* of 26 March 1877, brought to the fore the positive qualities of so many of Lench's Trustees:

> For nearly fifty years he had been prominent in Birmingham in every cause and work of a character to secure freedom, personal and political alike in thought and speech; to establish and strengthen good local government; to promote education in many varied forms, and in its best and widest sense; to help the neglected and the weak; and in all ways and at all times to make society better, purer, and wiser. Whenever projects for the social, moral, intellectual, or political progress of Birmingham were in question, Mr. Ryland was always to be found helping them, in his own hearty, sagacious, and unobtrusive way; and many a movement with which his name was not formally associated was greatly benefited by his wise counsel and practical guidance. Indeed, he did so much, and was so constantly engaged in public and semi-public business, that it is difficult to know where to begin the narrative of his labours.

Other prominent Unitarian Trustees were Hutton, the historian and by trade a stationer whose house was also attacked in 1791, and John Towers Lawrence, a hatter. Both were appointed in 1789, with Lawrence's son, a furrier, following in 1821. The younger man's involvement with Lench's spurred him into an incessant devotion to public work as a councillor, magistrate, supporter of the Birmingham and Midland Institute, and office holder with almost every social and charitable institution in the town. According to his obituary in 1871, "none of this was of his own seeking. By nature of a sensitive and retiring disposition, he never asked a favour for himself or courted popularity. But his fellow-citizens knew and appreciated his practical sagacity and high sense of honour, and he had far too high a conception of his duties as a citizen to shrink from accepting his fair share of

A portrait of William Hutton, a Unitarian Trustee of Lench's and the first person to write a history of Birmingham.

public work". That obituary could stand as a tribute to generations of Trustees. (*Birmingham Daily Gazette*, 10 May 1871).

Thomas Osler of the famed glass-making company on Broad Street was another Unitarian who became a Trustee in 1821. He too was followed by his sons, Thomas Clarkson, a friend of the poet Wordsworth, and the better-known Follett, who developed a way of building up solid glass around a metal core to create crystal objects of a size and complexity impossible before. With this method, Osler made a wondrous crystal fountain that was the magnificent centrepiece for the 1851 Great Exhibition. Over eight yards high and containing four tons of

Abraham Follett Osler, a Unitarian Trustee.

crystal, it seemed "a gorgeous stalactite from that concave sea of glass which gave translucent roofage to the great spectacle of human skill and toil". A man of many parts, Osler was passionately interested in opening education to working-class children. A key figure in setting up the National Education League which resulted in the 1872 Education Act, his campaigning was recognised by the name of Follett Osler School in Osler Street.

An enthusiast for chronometry, the scientific measurement of time, in 1842, he collected funds to set up a standard clock for Birmingham in the town centre. To regulate it, Osler provided a transit instrument and an astronomical clock for its rooftop observatory. Without telling anyone, he altered the clock from Birmingham Time to Greenwich Time.

Gradually, church and private clocks locally were adjusted to match it, so that Birmingham was ahead of the rest of the country in moving to a national standard time. Elected as a Fellow of the Royal Society in 1855, Osler retired from business in 1876 to devote himself to his scientific interests. The epitome of a generous Lench's Trustee, mostly anonymously, he gave thousands to worthy causes and presented the clock and bells for Big Brum at the Council House.

Vested a Trustee in 1833 and the owner of a cock-founding concern, Robert Martineau was yet another Unitarian making his mark positively on Lench's and Birmingham. A descendant of French Huguenots and from a wealthy Norfolk family, he moved to Birmingham to marry Jane Smith and was obviously influenced by her father, Samuel, a merchant and Trustee since 1805. His brother, Timothy Smith, was a significant business figure as co-partner in the

Eagle Foundry on Broad Street. One of Birmingham's most important industrial premises, it stood close to the modern Exchange Building.

George Jacob Holyoake, a celebrated Birmingham campaigner for working-class rights, was employed there in the early 1830s. He recalled Smith as "a Unitarian, a placid gentleman. The men were always glad when it fell to him to pay them, as he had a kindly word for them, and would sometimes make them small advances when the wages of the piece-workers fell low". By contrast his partner and fellow Unitarian, William Hawkes, was harsh, exacting and flint-hearted. A descendant of an early feoffee, he became a Trustee in 1841.

Active politically, Robert Martineau was mayor of Birmingham in 1841. His son, Sir Thomas, was a lawyer and mayor three times and his daughter, Susan, was an original member of Lench's Ladies' Committee, soon becoming its secretary. In 1895, Robert's grandson, Ernest, became a Trustee, holding that position until his death in November 1951, when he was succeeded by his own grandson Denis. Both men also served Birmingham with distinction as councillors and lord mayors.

The Unitarian Beales were equally as invested with both a sense of civic duty and commitment to Lench's in the long term. Given as a gentleman, William Beale was appointed a Trustee in 1833. Eight years later, he was joined by his son, Samuel, then also holding the office of mayor. A glass and lead merchant, he was

William John Beale with the top hat is seated with members of his family at his Edgbaston home.

one of the founders of the Birmingham and Midland Bank. Later chairman of the Midland Railway, an ironmaster, and MP for Derby, he became a prominent member of the Unitarian Church of the Messiah which straddled what is now the Black Sabbath Bridge on Broad Street.

Appointed in 1848, Samuel Beale's solicitor brother, William John, was married to Martha Phipson, from a Unitarian family closely related to the Rylands. Their son, Charles Gabriel Beale, became a Trustee in 1869. Another solicitor, he was a politician and Lord Mayor of Birmingham four times as well as the first Pro-Chancellor of the University of Birmingham. Beale's wife, Alice Kenrick, was from yet another leading Unitarian family in Birmingham. With his appointment in 1906, their son, Hubert Kenrick Beale, took the family's service for Lench's into the fourth generation and the twentieth century. A solicitor with his father's firm of Beale and Co., he was an active councillor, director of several companies, guardian of the Birmingham Assay Office, and assiduous worker for several charities.

Although various discriminatory laws against Non-Conformists were repealed from 1828, Unitarians still aroused the ire of bigots, particularly regarding their significance in one of Birmingham's most important institutions, Lench's Trust. Two years later, they were accused of only seeking power, having "gotten by trickery, the government of the Court Leet, and also Lench's Trust, into which they do not admit a single *churchman* – although the property is derived from a *churchman*, and they have to render up their accounts annually to the *church*". These were spurious and alarmist arguments. Lench himself was a Roman Catholic not an Anglican; there was no trickery in the Unitarian presence on the Trust; and half of the Trustees at the time were not Unitarians.

Such falsehoods reared up again in 1854. In a Council meeting, Joseph Allday, a domineering councillor, demanded investigations into the running of Birmingham's Trusts. In particular, he railed that for many years Lench's had been in the hands of the Unitarians. He went on to denounce the prevalent idea that Lench was "a good Unitarian, who left considerable property for the support of poor aged women professing that faith, and that he directed there should be 15 trustees, all Unitarians". Nothing came of Allday's attacks and thereafter, antagonism towards Unitarians faded away as religious tolerance spread and as some of them became significant political figures locally. Foremost amongst those was the Liberal, Joseph Chamberlain, who bestrode Birmingham's political stage like a colossus in the late nineteenth and early twentieth centuries. (*Birmingham Journal*, 29 May 1830 and 21 January 1854).

Born in 1836 in London, he was 18 when sent to Birmingham to keep an eye on his father's large investment in the Broad Street screw-making firm of his uncle, John Sutton Nettlefold. Chamberlain soon took over the commercial and financial side of a business that rapidly expanded to employ more than 2,500 workers. Like other Unitarians, he advocated for the education of the working class and taught at evening adult education classes. Increasingly drawn to politics, in 1869 Chamberlain was elected to the town council, the same year as he was appointed a Lench's Trustee.

Within a brief time, his dynamism drew to him a band of young, energetic, and sympathetic councillors and in 1873 he was chosen as mayor. Using that honorary position as if it were the role of a managing director, he launched a rapid programme of municipal socialism, taking Council control of the local water and gas companies amidst other initiatives. Returned as MP for Birmingham West in 1876, he became a controversial figure through the enormous influence he wielded on the national stage. Still, he never neglected Birmingham's interests. Largely responsible for the creation of the University of Birmingham in 1900, he was also one of the Trustees elected following the implementation of the 1882 Charity Commissioners Scheme.

M P FOR BIRMINGHAM.

Joseph Chamberlain, a Lench's Trustee, not long after he was elected as MP for Birmingham.

Chapter 6

The Nineteenth-Century Charity Commission Scheme

The 1882 Scheme & Trustees

Delving deeply into Birmingham's charities as part of their remit to publish a report on public charities in England and Wales, in 1828 the Charity Commissioners noted that there was a surplus in the Trust's bank of £610. This was unusual but was attributed to the falling in of leases.

Most of the remaining leases were for building terms and they too were soon to expire. That would increase Lench's income greatly to an estimated £1,500 a year between 1849 and 1852. In their report, the Commissioners fully approved of the way the Trustees applied their income. Their only suggestion was that in making payments to almswomen, specific distributions should name the charities relating to Colmore, Ward, Wrixham, and Scott so as to keep their names in remembrance.

The Trust's administration was then investigated in detail in July 1879, but not because of any religious bias or Unitarian domination. Instead, the inspection was carried out on behalf of the Charity Commission, a permanent board set up in 1853 to inquire into the management of charitable trusts. It was strengthened by subsequent legislation enabling the Commissioners to exercise certain powers relating to the removal and appointment of Trustees, the vesting of property, and the establishment of schemes for the administration of charitable trusts. Importantly, the Commissioners operated under the traditional doctrine of 'cy-pres', interpreting the administration of charities as closely as possible to the testator's intentions.

After inquiring into Lench's foundation, endowments, objects, and present circumstances, the inspector suggested only that its management and application would be improved under a Scheme of the Commissioners. This would simplify routine business procedures and remove some difficulties, especially regarding the qualifications of Trustees. A year later, the majority of them applied for such a scheme. It was followed by an Order by the Commissioners on 13 October 1882.

This entailed discharging four Trustees wishing to retire; appointing the remaining 11 Trustees with two Elective Trustees; vesting the Trust property in the Official Trustee of the Charitable Lands in trust for the Charity; and establishing a scheme for the future regulation of the Trust.

This scheme had a number of provisions. First, all the original charities and their endowments should be consolidated into Lench's Trust, thus losing the names of the other benefactors. Next, the number of Trustees was fixed at 17 in total, with four of them 'Representative' and 13 'Elective'. All of them had to be competent, resident in Birmingham or within a convenient distance, and ratepayers at an annual value of no less than £60. Each Trustee was subject to the consent of the Charity Commissioners under their Official Seal, and they were to hold office for life, subject to disqualification on bankruptcy or neglect to attend Trustee meetings for two years. Finally, the four Representative Trustees were to be appointed by the town council, but if this were not done within two months after the scheme was dated then the other Trustees would appoint them.

The General Purposes Committee of the Council chose the Mayor, Alderman William White, Alderman Richard Chamberlain, Alderman William Cook, and Councillor John Hardman. Despite his inclusion and the fact that his older brother, Joseph, was an existing Trustee who'd become an elective, Richard Chamberlain spoke strongly against the proposal when brought before the full council for approval. His apparent contrariness was explained by his 'great objection' to the Charity Commissioners ignoring the council in the management of a charity in which the council and people had an interest. Even though they had no reason to give notice of the scheme, he was angered he'd never seen it.

Alderman William White, one of the first Birmingham councillors appointed as Trustees of Lench's under the 1882 Scheme.

It's also likely that Chamberlain wanted the Trust to come under the full control of the council as another example of municipal socialism.

Other councillors supported his objections, but perhaps the most compelling opposition came from Alderman Jesse Collings who was angered that the high ratal valuation would exclude the working class from becoming Trustees.

Because of that and as the representatives of the people, he demanded that the council should be actively involved in the Trust's affairs. Given that no working-class women and many working-class men didn't have the vote, the argument that the council actually represented the people as a whole and not just those with the franchise was a dubious one. As it was, other councillors emphasised that Lench's was well managed and nothing came of either the objections or demands. Indeed, soon after this debate, Richard Chamberlain and his three fellow councillors accepted the office of Representative Trustees. They joined the 13 Elective Trustees. (*Birmingham Mail*, 6 February 1883).

Trust Officers

Instituted in 1628, the office of Bailiff was continued under the 1882 Scheme. Henceforth, though, at the February quarterly meeting and usually by seniority, the Trustees would choose two of them as Acting Bailiff ('Bailiff Lench') and Junior Bailiff. Invested with full powers for financial responsibilities, the bailiffs attended the Trust office weekly for various matters and consulted with the Clerk, a recent role that embraced those of Secretary and Treasurer. For many years, the Trustees kept their own minutes but given the legalities that property ownership entailed, increasingly they needed advice from a solicitor who also took responsibility for minute taking.

John Gill junior was the first Clerk noted in the records. An attorney living in Moor Street, as had Lench, he died in 1794. He was replaced by Thomas Lee, thus beginning a long business relationship between his firm and the Trust. A Unitarian whose father played a leading role in prosecuting the 1791 rioters and recovering damages for their victims, he was the senior partner of Lee and Shipman in Newhall Street. Resigning in 1823 because as a magistrate he could no longer continue as a solicitor, Lee was proud that in 34 years he'd only missed two Lench's meetings, the rest of which had been "most social and pleasant".

He was succeeded by his son, Thomas Eyre Lee, and after his death in 1852, his son-in-law and partner, Charles Best, took over legal duties. Another Unitarian and one of the leading solicitors in Birmingham, he was also appointed as the Trust's first Clerk with a salary for all the secretarial work he undertook. As such, he was the Trust's first paid official. After his retirement in 1883, his partner, Thomas Horton, filled the role. A prominent figure in the Birmingham Law Society, he was clerk to other charities and a trustee of the Muntz Trust's work supporting medical charities. With his death in 1894, Thomas Hawkes Russell became the representative of the firm of Messrs Lee, Russell and Terry as it now was. His grandfather, James Russell, was a surgeon and Trustee appointed in 1841 and his father, James the younger, was a doctor who joined the Trust seven years later.

The only other Trust official was the unpaid position of Surveyor of the estates, first recorded in the 1782 minutes as the Unitarian Michael Lakin the younger, himself a Trustee. From the 1760s, he was effectively acting as an estate agent, appearing in numerous newspaper adverts for property particulars often in association with Thomas Lee, an attorney at law and the father of the Trust's second solicitor. Lakin was succeeded in 1798 by Thomas Bolton, a rule maker and another prominent Unitarian. After his death in 1834, his position was taken by his co-religionist Joseph Wells Hornblower, an architect and surveyor, who was followed by his firm of Hornblower and Haycock. From 1874, John Bickerton Williams, an estate agent and auctioneer, and his son, Edward, were surveyors.

The next appointment in 1915 brought together the origins of the Trust and the role of Surveyor in the person of Ernest Lakin-Smith. He was a direct descendant of both Michael Lakin, the Trust's first Surveyor in 1782, and William Hawkes, one of the original feoffees in 1525.

Lakin-Smith represented Chesshire, Gibson, and Co., auctioneers, land, house and estate agents, and surveyors. Begun in Birmingham, it's the founding predecessor firm of DTZ Investors which today operates in Europe and Asia.

Taken at the Ravenhurst Street almshouses in 1925, on the left is Ernest Lakin-Smith, Lench's Surveyor. He was a direct descendant of both Michael Lakin, the Trust's first Surveyor appointed in 1782, and William Hawkes, one of the original feoffees in 1525. On the right, just before the tree is William Byng Kenrick. Appointed a Trustee in 1915, he carried on his Unitarian family's service to Lench's.

Chapter 7

The Estates

Moor Street Estate

The Estates surveyed were vital to the Trustees in providing the income to carry out Lench's wishes. It was an income that increased significantly from the late eighteenth century with Birmingham's rapid and spectacular growth triggering a high demand for building land leading to the development of most of Lench's estates. An exception was the small and always urban Moor Street Estate, including properties in Park Street and Shut Lane. It was even more exceptional because it included the site in Moor Street itself where Lench had lived.

A plan of the Moor Street Estate from Arthur Musgrove's history of the Trust in 1926. It includes the site of the Digbeth almshouses, bottom left. Later demolished and the site sold, it's shaded in pink as is Wrixham's house in Mercer Street, just above St. Martin's. So too are the holdings in Moor Street, stretching down to Park Street, and along to Shut Lane, which disappeared for the building of Moor Street Station.

COMPILED FROM W. WESTLEY'S SURVEY OF BIRMINGHAM. 1731.

The earliest lease for the Estate dated to 1671, when it was granted for 200 years, an excessively long term that was against the Trust's decree. Then still on the edge of Birmingham, by the mid-eighteenth century Moor Street was heavily built up and its narrowing towards the Bull Ring caused serious issues for traffic, a situation made worse by mounds of rubbish that weren't cleared. Other streets were as bad and to allow the problems to be dealt with, leading citizens pushed for legislation. They succeeded and in 1769 an Act was passed "for laying open and widening certain ways and passages within the Town of Birmingham, and for cleansing and lighting the streets, ways, lanes, and passages there, and for removing and preventing nuisances and obstructions therein". Fifty Street Commissioners were appointed. Having each to be worth £1,000, they were men of much wealth and included several Unitarian Trustees: James Jackson, Michael Lakin, Thomas Lawrence, William May, and Joseph Smith.

Several properties were demolished for the widening of Moor Street. A third Act passed in 1801 authorised the clearance of more houses, including some belonging to the Trust, which bought land in Handsworth with the proceeds. The Moor Street buildings were replaced with a Prison and Public Office for magistrates and town meetings. Birmingham's first real administrative building, from 1838 the Public Office was also used by councillors until the Council House was completed. Over the succeeding decades, the Trust sold or exchanged other properties in Moor Street for road widening and in the 1880s, its remaining buildings on the Estate were cleared. They included the Woolpack, lost to the "inexorable law of improvement" bemoaned the *Birmingham Mail*.

The demolition of the Woolpack removes one of the old landmarks of the town, and the whole of that portion of Moor Street will be set back 15 feet, and will be level with the new building which has already been erected in close contiguity. The history of the Old Woolpack is rich in traditions over which one might almost grow sentimental; and as its demise in its present form is so rapidly drawing near, it may be interesting to recapitulate a few of the most noteworthy features in connection with the inn … The first that is known of the Woolpack is that it was the residence of William Lenche, who died within its walls, and in them also made that will which has conferred such great and lasting benefits upon the town. The house itself forms part of what has become to be known as Lench's Trust. It did not then include all the present premises adjoining houses having been included in it, or it having been annexed to adjoining taverns. It is at the beginning of the 18th century that notice is first given of the Woolpack as an inn. About that time it was the resort of educated classes of the town, and it is known that it was frequented by Dr. Johnson,

Moor Street in the 1950s shortly before it was transformed by redevelopment. On the left and by the van is the 'new' Woolpack pub, standing on the site of William Lenche's house. In the background are the buildings of Spiceal Street in the Bull Ring.

the great lexicographer. From that time to the present the Woolpack has flourished, though others of its competitors gradually fell out of existence. It has throughout presented very much the same appearance, and bears the stamp of hoary antiquity. Internally this is still more so, there being much that is quaint in its construction; and the passages being of that intricate character which is always met with in old buildings.

With the opening of the Public Office, the Woolpack drew in magistrates, solicitors, barristers, aldermen, and councillors attending meetings. Best known for his development of the modern postal service, Sir Rowland Hill and friends also met at the Woolpack and in 1819 they established "The Society for Literary Improvement", a form of debating society. In the 1840s, the premises was frequented by many leading Liberal politicians and "many an excited debate on the vexed question of the Corn Laws took place in the smoke room". (*Birmingham Mail*, 21 February 1885).

"Phoenix like", a new hotel "more in accord with the spirit of the times" rose up on part of the old Woolpack's site, with the building work uncovering an ancient watercourse, now filled in. This was Hersum's Ditch, important when Moor Street was developed in the late twelfth or early thirteenth centuries as it was a boundary separating the rear of the properties from the Little Park of the lords of the manor, recalled in Park Street. Elsewhere on the Estate, the demolition of old buildings allowed the Trust to advertise building leases for 99 years between 1889 and 1892. Some land remained vacant, though, until 1908 when it was sold for £20,000 to the Great Western Railway to become part of the site of Moor Street Station.

Sparkbrook Estate

At almost five acres, the Sparkbrook Estate was also exceptional in remaining agricultural longer than the land closer to the Bull Ring. In 1830 it was described as "a messuage, with (work)shop, barn, stable, outbuildings, garden, and appurtenances", two closes of land, and a cottage. Leased at £30 a year, the tenant had to keep the premises in repair and cultivate the land in a husband-like manner. Still, it was recognised that considerable advantage was anticipated from parcelling the land into building leases, for which they were conveniently situated.

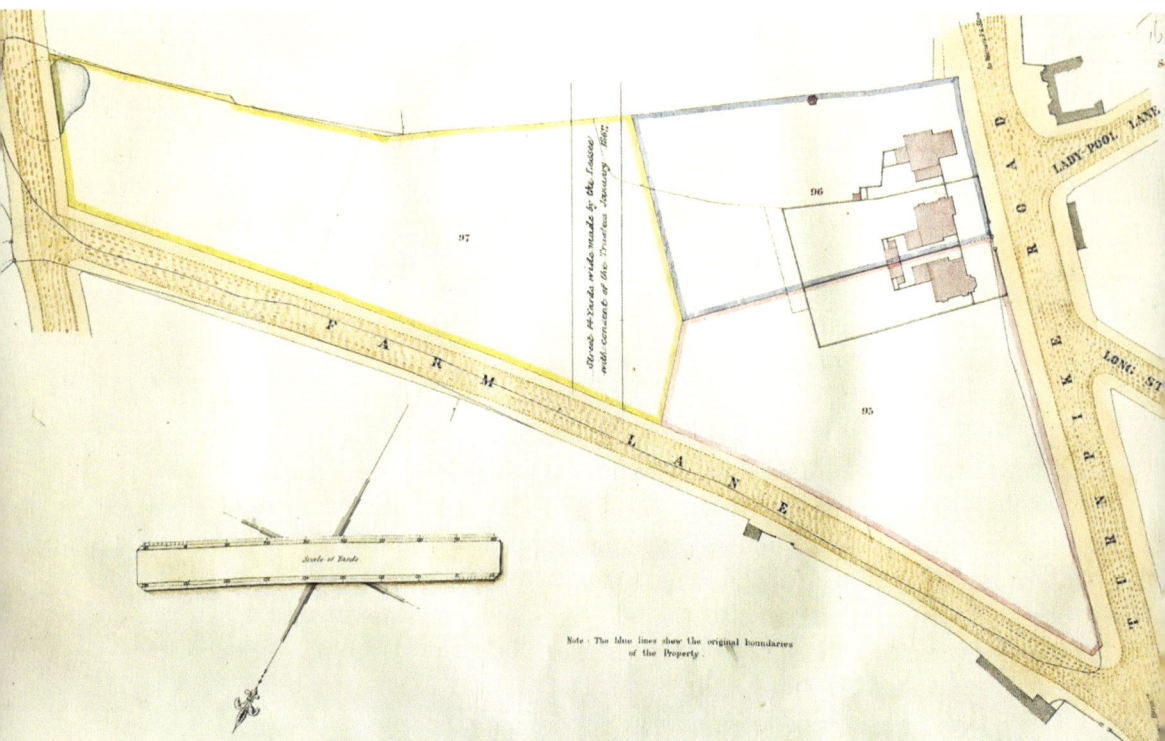

The Sparkbrook Estate when still rural. On the right, the Turnpike Road is the Stratford Road.

The Sparkbrook Estate in 1864 after its development with decent quality houses.

Just one and a half miles from the Bull Ring and easily reached on the main Stratford Road, the Estate was indeed a prime spot for development. That started in 1856, when it was let on three building leases for 99 years at a total rental of £130 per year. Within 11 years, the upper section of Gladstone Road was cut, and Farm Road was widened. Lying as it did in what was becoming a middle-class enclave around Farm Park, the development of the Estate was further marked out by the erection of 43 large houses rather than the back-to-backs for the poor that characterised the urbanisation of the other estates.

By the 1930s, however, the neighbourhood was surrounded by factories and working-class streets, whilst the houses once sought after by the aspiring middle class were now old-fashioned, draughty, cold, and difficult to maintain compared to the newly built, more modern homes in emerging suburbs like nearby Hall Green. Encouraged by these push and pull factors, middle-class families began to move away, a flight hastened by the Blitz on Birmingham and the bombing of the nearby BSA. After the Second World War, many of their former homes were turned into lodging houses for Irish, West Indian, and South Asian newcomers coming to the city to help rebuild it physically and economically. With a deteriorating housing stock, this part of Sparkbrook was soon regarded as "a twilight area" and in 1967, the council bought much of Lench's properties for £8,500. (*Birmingham Daily Post*, 3 February 1967).

St. Mary's Estate

Taking its name from the local Anglican church, now gone, the St. Mary's Estate covered Hawke's Croft, one of Lenche's gifts, and Loveday Croft. The first buildings were almshouses erected in 1688 on the corner of Steelhouse Lane and Lancaster Street. They were demolished in 1764, when, apart from a small plot for new almshouses, much of the land was taken on building leases by Joseph Taylor for 99 years. This length of term drew the attention of the commissioners on charitable foundations in 1828. They noted that whilst the decree of 1628 restricted leases to 21 years that constraint could not have been intended to apply to building leases. Even so, terms of 99 years were longer than generally met with, "but not more so than the custom of this part of the country appears to warrant, or the special circumstances of the case may be presumed to have required". Importantly, the Trust's mode of letting was approved: vacant premises were examined by a competent surveyor and the terms of each lease were made according to his estimation of their value.

During the early years of Taylor's tenure, Loveday Street, Lench Street, Bailey Street, Russell Street, and Price Street were cut. Additionally, the upper part of Walmer Lane was renamed Lancaster Street, where Taylor was covenanted to build at least "three or more substantial dwelling-houses, three-storeys high, fronting to and ranging with Lench's-row, and also to lay open a street, eight yards wide at the least". It was apparent that the Trustees wanted to ensure the quality of structures by requiring the spending of at least £1,000 on the buildings and the making of a public street. A variety of other building leases were granted to different tenants between 1778 and 1785, some with terms of up to 106 years.

On the expiration of Taylor's lease in 1864, the properties he'd built were leased as blocks for the shorter term of 21 years to various tenants having the responsibility of repairs. Eleven years later, the whole Estate was scheduled as part of a wider unhealthy district and included in the Birmingham Improvement Scheme. This was Joseph Chamberlain's grandiose plan to clear old buildings and replace them with Corporation Street, a Parisian-style boulevard flanked with impressive structures reflecting the town's status as the metropolis of the Midlands. The Trustees agreed a sale for £41,708, but the scheme was reduced in scope. In the end, the council purchased only a block on the corner of Bailey Street and Steelhouse Lane, and a strip of land for widening the latter.

However, as most of the houses on the Estate were in a deplorable state, the Trustees agreed to demolish them when the leases expired. As it was, they managed to obtain surrenders to allow the clearance of all the properties and the making of the new Vesey Street between Lench Street and Price Street. In 1892, most of the former Hawkes Croft was sold to the Committee responsible for building a new General Hospital, now the Children's Hospital. In return, the Trust received £11,000 and several houses in Loveday Street, later buying the adjoining properties for £2,100. Elsewhere on the Estate, between 1888 and 1921, the Trust offered leases for terms of 99 years for "eligible building sites". Taken up gradually, they were covered with substantial structures. The remaining vacant land fronting Lancaster Street was bought in 1925 by the council for £3,493 for road widening.

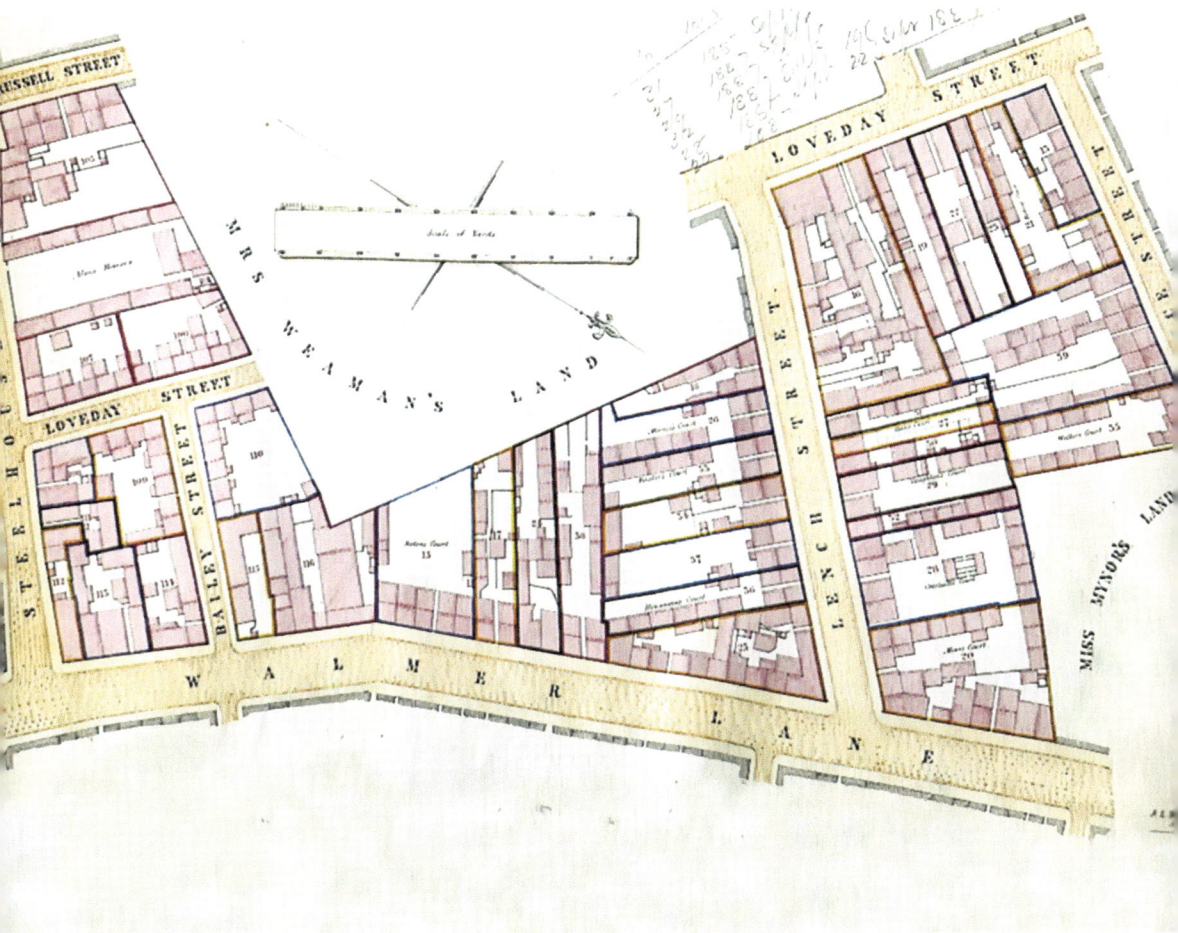

A plan of the St. Mary's Estate in 1864 before many of the properties were cleared. It makes plain the dominance of back-to-backs like those on Russell Street (top left). There are also blind backs. These were houses with a back wall with no windows or doors but with no other dwelling behind them, such as those off Lench Street (bottom right).

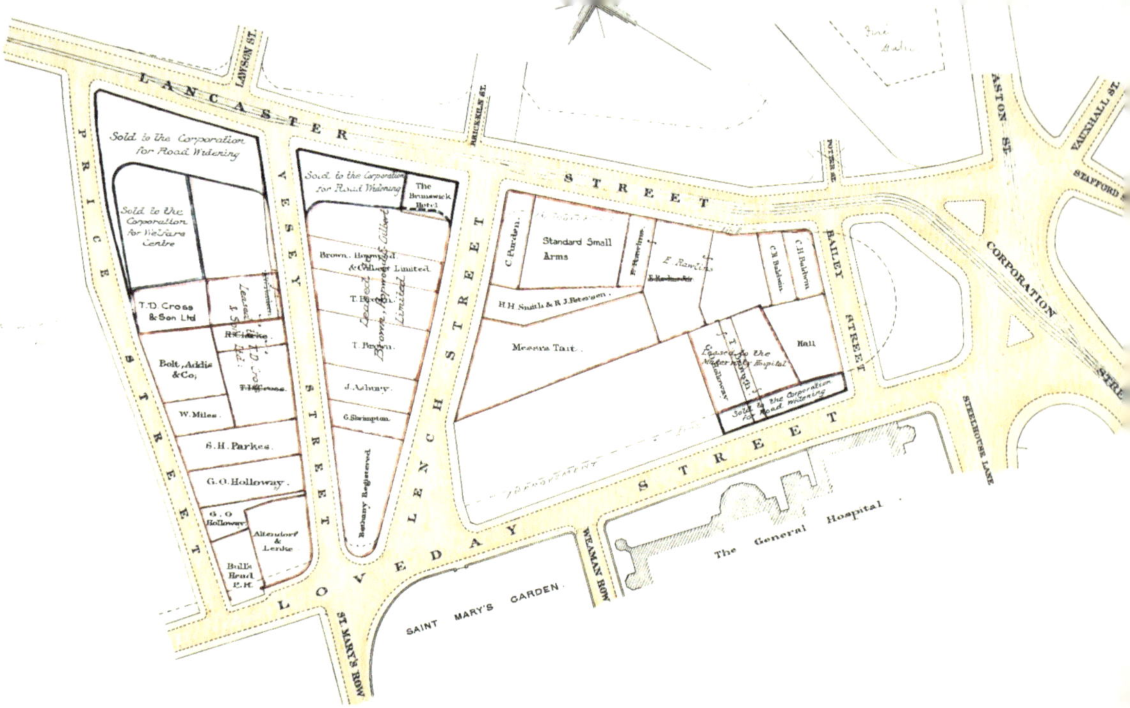

A plan of the St. Mary's Estate in 1901 after the clearance of its slum properties and indicating the land sold and leased for the building of modern commercial structures.

The corner of Lench Street (left) and Lancaster Street in the 1930s showing some of the new buildings put up since the clearance of insanitary properties.

Woodcock Croft Estate

Brought into Lench's officially in 1628, the Woodcock Croft Estate took its name from a bird with brownish feathers, short legs, and a long, thin beak. Living mainly in woods, it was sometimes hunted for food or sport. Like the St. Mary's Estate, it fell before the outpouring of Birmingham and in 1752, the Croft was leased for 99 years to John Rann, a member of a long-established family locally. Having paid £20 and agreeing to spend £400 on building, he put up 17 front houses and shops in Prospect Row and 53 front houses and 21 back houses in Woodcock Street. This development still left a considerable extent of vacant land upon which a clay pit was dug. It was one of many around expanding Birmingham, as the clay was fired into the town's distinctive red bricks. Like other pits, when exhausted it was filled in and built upon, in this case with Potter Street.

The Woodcock Croft Estate was enlarged by the Trustees but then diminished with the council purchasing land in 1847 for the Duke Street Police Station and six years afterwards, for Woodcock Street Baths. After Rann's leases fell in, the Trustees re-let the shops and granted leases for the Woodcock Street houses for 21 years with the tenants responsible for repairs. They were leased again on the same terms in 1872. A remaining sizeable portion of vacant land was developed for widening Brueton's Walk and making it Brueton Street and for cutting Lower Lawrence Street. Plots alongside these were quickly let on building leases.

Like the St. Mary's Estate, the Woodcock Croft Estate was scheduled for clearance in the Birmingham Improvement Scheme but was withdrawn. Writing in 1926, Arthur Musgrove, Lench's clerk, explained that for many years, the houses were farmed out to lessees who'd let them get into such a state of disrepair that they'd been certified by the Medical Officer of Health. In 1893, when the leases reached their terms, the Trustees only renewed the Prospect Row shops, instead taking over and managing the houses themselves on weekly rents. Musgrove felt that this was "by reason of a feeling on their part that the responsibility of the upkeep of the property should be borne by them as the owners of the estate and should no longer be handed over to lessees some of whom might not fulfil their obligations. No doubt this was owing to the greater interest in the housing question which was taken about that period. A considerable sum of money was spent on opening courts and repairing the property …" That was a rather optimistic assessment as in 1901, the Trust was rocked by claims that it managed 'slum property'.

Birmingham's burgeoning population fuelled a rapidly rising demand for housing, with jerry builders taking over any unbuilt land on the town's outskirts,

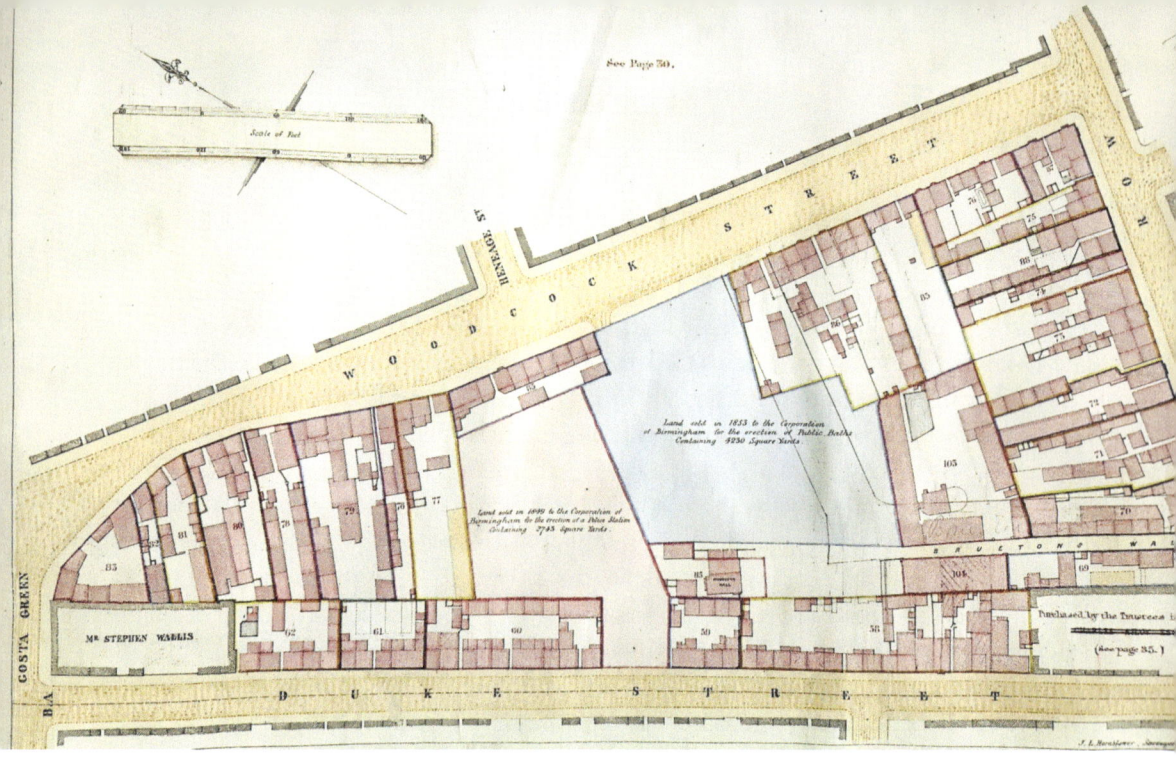

The Woodcock Street Estate in 1864. The land in pink and blue was sold to the council for the building of Duke Street Police Station and Woodcock Street Baths. Again, the presence of back-to-backs and blind backs is obvious.

such as in and around Woodcock Street, and filling it with badly-built back-to-backs. Usually erected on impure foundations and built shoddily with inferior materials such as dirt instead of sand for the mortar, a back-to-back was one of a terrace of houses at the back of which was another dwelling belonging to another terrace. Thus, the two houses shared a dividing wall, merely one brick in depth, meaning that there were no back doors or windows. Consequently, there was a lack of light and no through ventilation.

All back-to-backs had a small 15 foot square room downstairs which was multi-purpose, having to serve as a living room, dining room, kitchen, washroom, workroom, and sometimes a bedroom. Cooking was on a range or latterly, on a cooker placed in a tiny scullery with a crock sink and a few shelves. Sometimes there was also a cellar in which coke and wood were kept for fuel. The flooring of the all-encompassing room downstairs was quarry tiles covered by peg rugs made by women bodging (stitching) old rags onto urden (hessian) sacking. Many back-to-backs were two-storeys high, meaning that there were two small bedrooms above the one room downstairs. However, a large number of back-to-backs were attic high, which gave extra sleeping space by having one bedroom above another.

Long terraces of back-to-backs dominated street after street in much of Birmingham. Between four or more of these front houses there was an entry

A back yard in Woodcock Street in the 1930s, when Lench's began to demolish its back-to-backs, as shown here. At the bottom is the communal brew'us as Brummies called the washhouse and in the foreground is a miskin, dustbin.

leading to what officials called a court, but which was known by working-class Brummies as a yard. This gave access to the houses behind the terrace fronting to the street and normally to another terrace of back-to-backs running along the yard at right angles to the entry. The houses backing onto these faced into another yard. Each yard was a shared space with communal facilities, including the washing line and brew'us (washhouse) with a copper (boiler) set in brick and below which was space to light a fire to heat the water in the copper. The yard also had an area for the ashes and rubbish called the miskins, and lavatories, one of which was shared between two or more families.

The dreadful state of the back-to-backs in Woodcock Street was pulled into the public glare in 1901 in a series of searing articles in the *Birmingham Daily Gazette* written by its lead writer, J. Cuming Walters. Called 'Scenes in Slumland: Pen Pictures of the Black Spots in Birmingham', his revelations about the extent of poverty and "slum landlordism" in the "best governed city in the world" caused an outcry. He highlighted one very narrow court in Woodcock Street that was made more of a death-trap than before because the authorities had allowed a large

A steep yard opened by the Trust by knocking down the two properties which had faced the street and the two behind them. This action was taken after the revelations in 'Scenes in Slumland'. The photo was taken in the 1930s, not long before these properties were demolished. Notice the efforts made by the local women to stay clean and respectable: the line of clean washing at the top of the yard and the mother showing her baby her window box of flowers.

timber structure to be erected at the entrance. If there were a fire and the flames spread "the inhabitants, probably to the number of 50, would be penned in and roasted alive, without a chance of escape". In a nearby court, "a perfectly new bricked-in place for manure has been built in front of the houses and there was the manure smoking and poisoning the air with its fumes as we passed by". Yet another court was approached by an entry so steep that it was difficult to walk down it steadily without slipping. ('Scenes in Slumland', *Birmingham Daily Gazette*, 26 June 1901).

In his walks through the wretched streets of this part of 'Slumland', Cuming Walters was told several times that certain bad property belonged to Alderman William Cook, the chairman of the Council's Health Committee. Enraged, he took out a libel action, in which the origins of the rumours about his ownership emerged. After the report on the wooden structure in the Woodcock Street court, Cook went to see it in his position as Bailiff of Lench's because a notice of removal was served on the Trust as its owner. It was then revealed that Cuming Walters had also highlighted slum properties belonging to the Trust in Garrison Lane (Callow Fields) and Loveday Street amongst others.

Whilst condemning Cook for his involvement, the *Gazette* acknowledged that he gave his time to Lench's in the interests of the homes for women it maintained. This was most honourable and praiseworthy service, as was that he also rendered as Bailiff of King Edward's Grammar School, which "sorry to say that that great public foundation is not wholly free from the reproach of owning property to which it would be well if the attention of the Sanitary Authority were more frequently directed". Still, the question was asked: "While such Trusts and Foundations own property in streets of the lowest sanitary class, is it right that a person connected with them as one of a number of Trustees should hold a perpetual chairmanship of the Health Committee?" ('Alderman Cook and Lench's Trust', *Birmingham Daily Gazette*, 7 November 1901).

In its early building leases, the Trust insisted on substantial structures, but it seems that a lack of oversight in the mid-nineteenth century allowed sub-lessees to build shoddy and unhealthy back-to-backs. Stung into action, the Trust embarked on the rapid renovation of the Woodcock Croft Estate. As Musgrove observed, a considerable sum was spent on opening courts and repairing the property which was then kept in a proper state. Some were demolished in the mid-1930s when land was sold for building the new Central Fire Station, whilst the rest were cleared when the council took over the rest of the Estate as part of Birmingham's post-Second World War redevelopment. Today much of the former Woodcock Croft Estate is part of Aston University's site.

Trust properties in Duke Street, part of the Woodcock Croft Estate, in 1967. Not long afterwards, they were pulled down and Duke Street disappeared.

Callow Fields Estate

The revelations in 'Scenes in Slumland' also spurred the Trust into the rapid clearance of slum housing on the Callow Fields Estate. At nine acres, it was the largest of the estates and the records of Bordesley Manor indicated that it was in Lenche's family before he took over. By the early nineteenth century, it was divided into three fields and with a hovel the only building, it was bounded by the upper part of Garrison Lane (then Green Lanes), Watery Lane, and the farm of John Jukes. In 1811, he leased the Estate for building purposes for a term of 99 years. After the first 10, he'd pay a rental of £137 14s 4d, whilst he covenanted to spend £3,000 on new properties and insure them against fire for a further £3,000. Instead, he cut Witton Street and Saltley Street and from 1813, he sub-let plots to different builders.

The Callow Fields Estate in 1864 when back-to-backs and blind backs were still set amidst open land and gardens.

Six years later, he sold his leasehold to the Birmingham Blue Coat School, then a charitable institution for teaching poor children. By 1828, the Estate had 86 front and 47 back houses. Musgrove indicated that from a survey undertaken by the Trust in 1833 "it is evident that this was a very deserving attempt to make a small garden city". Depicted in colours, the plan showed each house having a garden with trees, flowers, and vegetable beds. Unfortunately, within a few years the idea of a garden city was unthinkable as terrace after terrace of back-to-backs were thrown up by jerry builders. (*Aris's Birmingham Gazette,* 4 January 1830).

By the later nineteenth century, the Callow Fields Estate was regarded as a very poor insanitary area with dreadful living conditions. So bad was the situation that in April 1896 the Trustees were summoned before the magistrates to explain why a closing order on seven houses in Lower Dartmouth Street should not be made. Dr. Hill, Birmingham's Medical Officer of Health, said that on a recent inspection, they were damp, dilapidated, and unfit for habitation. The solicitor representing Lench's explained that the houses were leased, and that the leaseholder was informed of the proceedings but hadn't attended. In response, he was told that it was to the Trust's advantage that the premises were kept in proper condition, whilst the law required proceedings be taken against the freeholders and for them to settle with the leaseholders. Accordingly, the order was made to close the premises. (*Birmingham Mail,* 24 April 1896).

Increasingly concerned at the deplorable state of housing on the Estate and the lack of care of the Blue Coat School administrators, in 1901, Lench's approached the Charity Commissioners to allow an agreement for the school to surrender its lease on payment of £650 for dilapidations. With that achieved, the Trust then went on to demolish over 200 houses, leaving only a few that were better built in Lower Dartmouth Street. The five acres of cleared land was advertised for building leases, but there were no takers. However, aware that councillors were looking for spaces to make recreation grounds in overcrowded poorer neighbourhoods, in 1910 the Trustees offered the site to the council with a price of £5,000.

In pushing to accept, one councillor explained that this was precisely the sum which "would have had to be capitalised one hundred years ago when the land was let for building". Lench's was willing to accept this amount simply because the council wanted it for useful purposes. The offer was accepted as there was an urgent need for breathing space in a congested district with general death and infant mortality rates amongst the highest in the city. (*Birmingham Daily Gazette,* 8 June 1910).

At a cost of £2,334 the ground was levelled and divided into two sections. One was laid out as a park, with trees, gravel paths, bandstand, and bowling green. Separated by non-climbable railings along the line of the former Saltley

Lower Dartmouth Street in 1952 with the Callow Fields Recreation Ground on the right. Now owned by the council, the site had been in William Lenche's family since at least the late fifteenth century.

Street, the other was for children. Levelled, rolled, and drained, its main path from Watery Lane divided the boys' playground from the girls'. Both had swings, remained open until 9pm, and were illuminated in the winter with electric lights. Boasting an attendants' room, public shelter, and drinking fountain, Callow Fields Recreation Ground was officially opened by the Lord Mayor on 8 October 1912, with hundreds of children rushing in as soon as he did so. It was also called Garrison Lane Recreation Ground but was better known locally as Itchy Coo Park. Perhaps taken from the Scots word for anything tickling children, it may relate to the number of big sisters minding the babies in their families in the 'Rec'. (*Birmingham Mail*, 7 October 1912).

Brass Street Estate

Coming into the Trust in 1668 as a croft, the short and narrow Brass Street was cut out by one of the lessees and never dedicated officially as a public highway. The smallest of the Estates, it ran between Newtown Row (originally Walmer Lane) and Summer Lane and was squashed betwixt Theodore Street and Moorsom Street, formerly Harding Street and notorious for its slogging gang and peaky blinders in the nineteenth century. Its development was heralded in 1752 when

John Rann took on a building lease, but after 44 years, he'd only put up two houses, prompting the Trustees to pay him £130 to surrender his interest.

Following an intermediary lease, in 1825 the estate was let to Edward Lightwood for 99 years. Keen to ensure suitable development, the Trustees required him to spend at least £1,000 "erecting substantial messuages upon the said piece of land, and to maintain in good repair the messuages then built, and such as thereafter should be built thereon, and to insure the messuages built against fire to the value of £1,000 at the least". Within three years, he'd partially fulfilled those conditions with two front houses, a manufactory, and 17 back houses. It seems that the lease was then sold to Josiah Pumphrey who built 16 more back houses with large gardens and five dwellings facing Summer Lane which later became shops. Some open land remained but after the lease was sold again in 1849, this and the gardens soon disappeared. (*Aris's Birmingham Gazette*, 29 January 1849).

As with the back-to-backs of Callow Fields and Woodcock Street, those of Brass Street deteriorated badly and were quickly enveloped in a stifling environment. In his devastating reports of 1901, Cuming Walters revealed that the two courts of houses were curiosities, showing what could be done in a small area "if only the builder is ingenious and the city authorities are half asleep". The

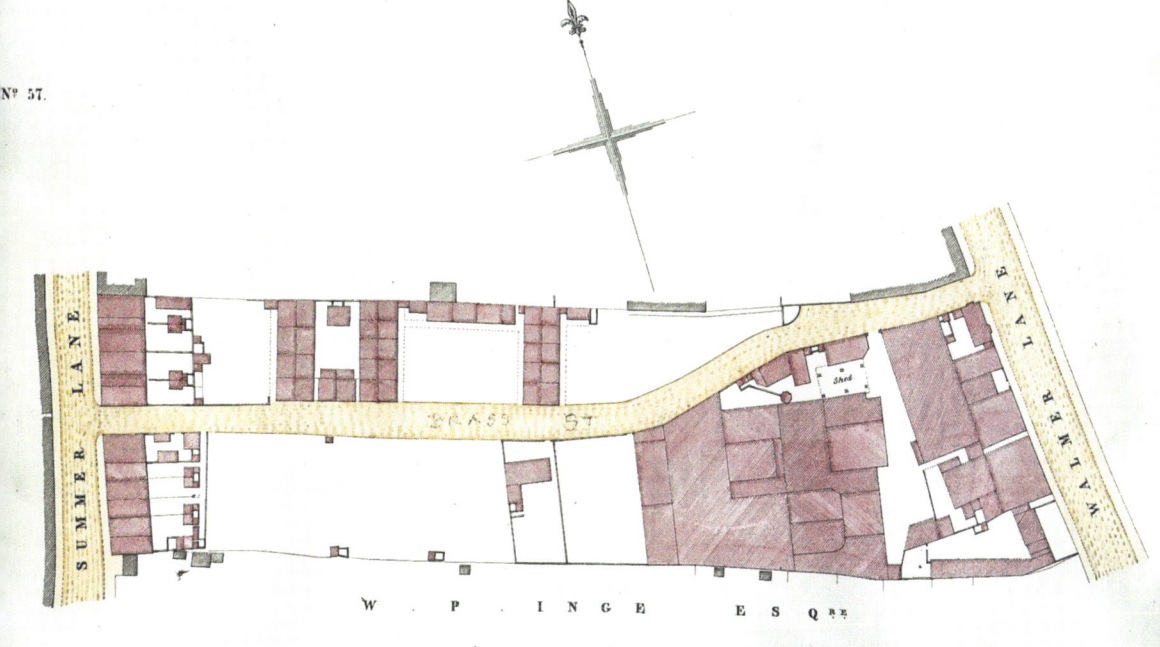

The Brass Street Estate in 1864, showing the back-to-backs on the north side.

first was "a narrow, miserable, vilely-smelling place, which, we learn is 'much improved' from what it was. Heaven only knows what it was, then, before the improvement was effected". There were three small and dejected-looking houses with their residents looking upon a high wall just feet away from their doors.

Things were even worse in Court 2, for at its top "you are amazed to find that at right angles to it is merely a gullet (narrow passageway) leading to another row of houses, practically hidden from sight by the tall hoardings of a timber yard". Scarcely a ray of light or breath of fresh air could come here, the owner of the timber yard having gained permission to close in the houses with a high wooden wall that left only just enough room to walk in and out. It was a despairing spectacle with the wretched dwellers in the gullet having everything taken from them that could make life pleasant and healthy. A few years later, number 2 Court Brass Street featured in a graphic photographic survey of the worst housing in Birmingham.

All the Brass Street properties reverted to the Trust in 1924 and the manufactory and some of the houses were re-let for 21 years to John Reynolds and Sons, manufacturers of nails, who'd held the old lease for many years.

Dreadful living conditions in Brass Street's back-to-backs at the turn of the twentieth century. (Library of Birmingham)

Musgrove stated that Lench's then invested a considerable expenditure in repairs on the rest of the properties. These shops, houses, and stabling were let on either 24-year or short tenancies.

Until the mid-1950s, a cast-iron nameplate stood at the corner of Brass Street and Newtown Row and "only a few of those who notice it are likely to realise that the name it bears – Lench's Trust – indicating the ownership of neighbouring property, is that of one of the oldest charitable institutions of its kind in the country". The nameplate was near to a group of partly demolished houses, the harbinger of the clearance of all the buildings and the disappearance of Brass Street itself in Birmingham Council's post-1945 redevelopment of its central districts. (*Birmingham Daily Post*, 13 January 1956).

In addition to its main estates, by 1901, Lench's owned a few properties in Princip Street, the Horsefair, Dale End, the Jewellery Quarter, and a larger number in Moseley. These were on the Wake Green Road near to St. Mary's Row; around Caroline Road and close to the Alcester Road; and on the Kingswood Estate, off Church Road as it led to the Ladypool Road.

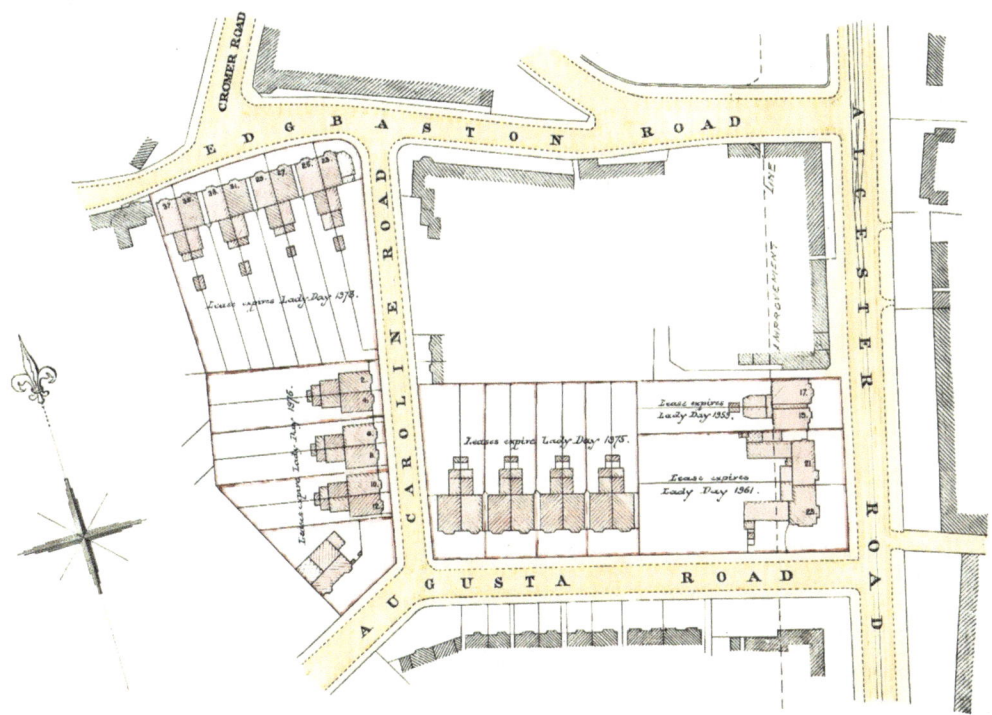

Above, Lench's properties around Caroline Road, Moseley, on the border with Balsall Heath and with the Alcester Road to the east.

Chapter 8

The Trust in Action

Bridge Repairs

In their Declaration of Trust in 1540, the Trustees made it clear that the rents and profits from the Estates should be distributed first to repair the ruined ways and bridges in and about Birmingham where there was need. As an unincorporated town, Birmingham lacked a council and, as previously discussed, the only authorities with some form of local government were the justices, constables, and high and low bailiffs of the Leet. To these could be added Lench's Trust because of its importance in connecting Birmingham via bridges over the River Rea to roads leading to Coventry, Warwick, and Stratford, and thence further south and to London. As a landlocked town, it was vital that merchants could send out manufactured goods and that would be impossible if there were no bridges and merely a ford impassable in flooding. This reality was obviously a major reason why notable men sought the position of Trustee. It was not only prestigious, confirming their status, but it also gave them power.

The importance of the bridges was highlighted by the Commissioners in 1628 when they upbraided the Trustees for not repairing those over the Rea at Deritend. Their failure to do so may have been impacted by the increasing tensions in England between the supporters of Charles I and Parliament, leading not only to the Civil War but also to a focus on political matters. Or else, as suggested in the Inquisition, it may have resulted from the seven remaining Trustees looking after each other's interests more than their duties. Whatever the cause, thereafter it seems that better care was taken of this bridge as well as others elsewhere across the river and also over the Hockley Brook. These repairs along with those for Birmingham's roads were made under the direction of the Trust's bailiffs. Writing in 1880, Robert K. Dent stressed the importance of their roles in disbursing funds.

> Gravel and stones were purchased and brought from Winson Green, and carters, labourers, and paviours were constantly employed.
>
> At times a paviour had to be brought from Lichfield or other distant places.

Timber was largely used in staking up the rude footpaths, and now and again a bridge was washed away in a flood. The badly-made roads were, in hilly situations such as Digbeth and Carr's Lane, easily destroyed by heavy rains, the functions, therefore, of the bailiff assimilated to those of the modern borough surveyor, and he shared the official importance of the town bailiff and constable.

Contract work was unknown, every job was ordered and paid for in detail, even to the ale which was an invariable accompaniment to the work.

The wooden bridges over the Rea were barred and kept chained and locked by an attendant bar-keeper. In the later seventeenth century, they were replaced by a stone bridge paid for by the town surveyors appointed by the lord of the manor. Over the next century, this and other bridges over the Rea and also the River Tame came under the control of highway trusts. With bridges no longer their remit, Lench's continued repairing roads and in 1761 a notice appeared in the local newspaper from Robert Moore, Bailiff:

Whereas Digbeth Street in this Town has been often represented to the Trustees of Lench's Lands as very dangerous to travel through on Horseback, or otherwise, and that if there was a Land (proper horse road) made in the middle of the said Street, it would be much more safe, and of publick Utility, not only to the Inhabitants of this Town, but to all others, who shall have Occasion to travel through the same; and as several persons have already offered to subscribe to this great and useful Undertaking; this is therefore to acquaint the Public that as soon as a sum of Money shall be raised proper to begin such an Undertaking, that the said Trustees are willing to do all in their Power to compleat it, not leaving undone such other things as they are bound to do under their Trust. (*Aris's Birmingham Gazette*, 6 April 1761).

From 1769, the Street Commissioners were responsible for repairing streets and bridges, but with their income mostly spent on demolishing obstructive buildings, the Trustees continued with their historical role. Its importance was highlighted in 1817 when the local newspaper reported that Lench's Trust was attending to the bad state of Pinfold Street by its property, and it was hoped that the Trustees would extend the improvement to the whole street. Considerable sums of money continued to be spent by the Trustees on road repairs, and in 1829, it was reported that they were either advanced to the Commissioners upon their application for specific projects or were expanded by the Trustees themselves where they thought it was needed. Over the previous five years, the average disbursement was £227 14 shillings.

However, the incorporation of Birmingham as a municipal borough in 1838 gave the council the authority to cover public works and the Trust's involvement in street repairs diminished noticeably. It finally ended in 1846 with a contribution to the repair of Old Meeting Street. Thereafter, Lench's focused its attention on the upkeep of its almshouses and on benefitting the women living in them. (*Aris's Birmingham Gazette*, 4 January 1830).

Deritend Bridge in 1932, long after it was no longer the responsibility of Lench's.

'Gifts' to the Poor & the First Almshouses

In their Declaration of 1540, the Trustees stated that in default of the primary aim of repairing bridges and roads, they could bestow their income upon the poor where there was the greatest want. It's not known how they did so, although Wrixham's bequest willed that the rents and profits from his building should be distributed annually on Good Friday. After his charity became part of Lench's in 1628, the Trustees carried on doing so until the end of the eighteenth century. In 1789, the Minutes recorded that "it would be better if the practice of going about the streets on Good Friday and giving money to poor persons mostly unknown to the Trustees was discontinued". This was because the money handed out was of little utility and frequently was used badly. It was resolved to end the practice and instead the money should be endowed to the almshouses in Steelhouse Lane.

As Musgrove discerned, it was apparent that some of the elder Trustees "were loath to give up their accustomed Good Friday walks distributing largesse". Keen to keep their public display of charity manifesting their power and prestige, the next year it was resolved that in future, the Bailiff should have 12 guineas to divide amongst the six senior Trustees to distribute amongst the poor as they saw fit. As each one of them died, their share ceased to be allotted, with the custom ending in 1802. Thereafter, no payments were made to the poor outside the Trust's almshouses.

There are no photographs or drawings of the Digbeth almshouses, but they were endowed about the same time as those of Sir Thomas Holte in the mid-seventeenth century. This photo shows Eliza Cooper, née Roe, outside 3 almshouse Aston Lane. Born in 1837 in Lincolnshire, she came to Birmingham where she married John Cooper, a brewer. After his death, she was left with a 12-year-old son and daughter aged 10. Having to take in a lodger to help her get by, she went on to become a monthly nurse. She carried on doing so at least until she was 74 and in Holte's almshouse. Eliza was the kind of woman who would have found a place at Lench's. Thanks to Lynn Schuck, her great-great-granddaughter.

The first of these were in Digbeth. In his monumental work on English Guilds, Toulmin Smith found documentary evidence that the Guild of the Holy Cross had four almshouses for poor men and women who'd been members. They lived rent free as did poor people who weren't formerly in the guild in other almshouses. It's not known where these buildings were; however, Toulmin Smith believed they were in Digbeth and that somehow, they survived the dissolution of the guild and came into Lench's. Yet they were not mentioned in the 1628

Inquisition and although noted in the accounts 11 years later, they weren't specifically included in a legal document until 1691. In these circumstances, Robert K. Dent's dating is more plausible. He felt that the Digbeth almshouses were put up by the Trust itself about the same time as those endowed by Sir Thomas Holte in the mid-seventeenth century.

These Digbeth almshouses on the corner of Allison Street were pulled down in 1726 because they were "so ruinous and out of repair that they were ready to fall down". They were replaced on the same site with eight dwelling houses. The 12 poor people living in them were enjoined to do so quietly, peaceably, and not "suffer any other person (other than their own families) to come and dwell with them". These residents included four men and their wives, two single men, and two unmarried women. Only two of them could sign their name. The Digbeth almshouses were demolished in 1764 and the land advertised for building leases.

In 1688, the Trustees paid for the building of another set of almshouses on the corner of Steelhouse Lane and Walmer Lane, later Lancaster Street. Over 44,600 bricks were bought for 22 shillings and 6 pence (just over £1), and Henry Cooks and Job Crowley were paid almost 6 shillings (30p) to lay them. The finished almshouses were then on the edge of Birmingham in a semi-rural location brought into view by Dent.

> From their doors or windows, the inmates could enjoy one of the fairest prospects of which our delightful county (Warwickshire) could boast, even in those early days, when black, smoking chimneys were fewer, and the limits of the domain of brick and mortar much more confined than nowadays. Away on the left could be seen in the distance the gently rising eminence of Barr-beacon … Nearer, and rather more to the right, would be seen the minaret-crowned towers of Aston Hall, and the tall, graceful spire of the pretty village church, rising from the midst of a grove of trees; still further to the right, (almost in the middle of the prospect,) the village of Erdington, crowning the little eminence called Gravelly Hill, and behind it the well-wooded park of Sutton Coldfield; and away to the right might then be seen the beautiful spire of Coleshill Church. This almshouse was indeed a pleasant harbour of refuge for the aged poor, weary and worn with the battle of life, where they might end their days in peaceful retirement, away from the busy hive in which they had toiled during their earlier years.
>
> But the town grew, and ere long surrounded the little group of almshouses; the furnaces of Kettle's steel-houses sent forth smoke to cloud the prospect, and, by and by, rows of houses sprang up in Walmer Lane to block it out altogether.

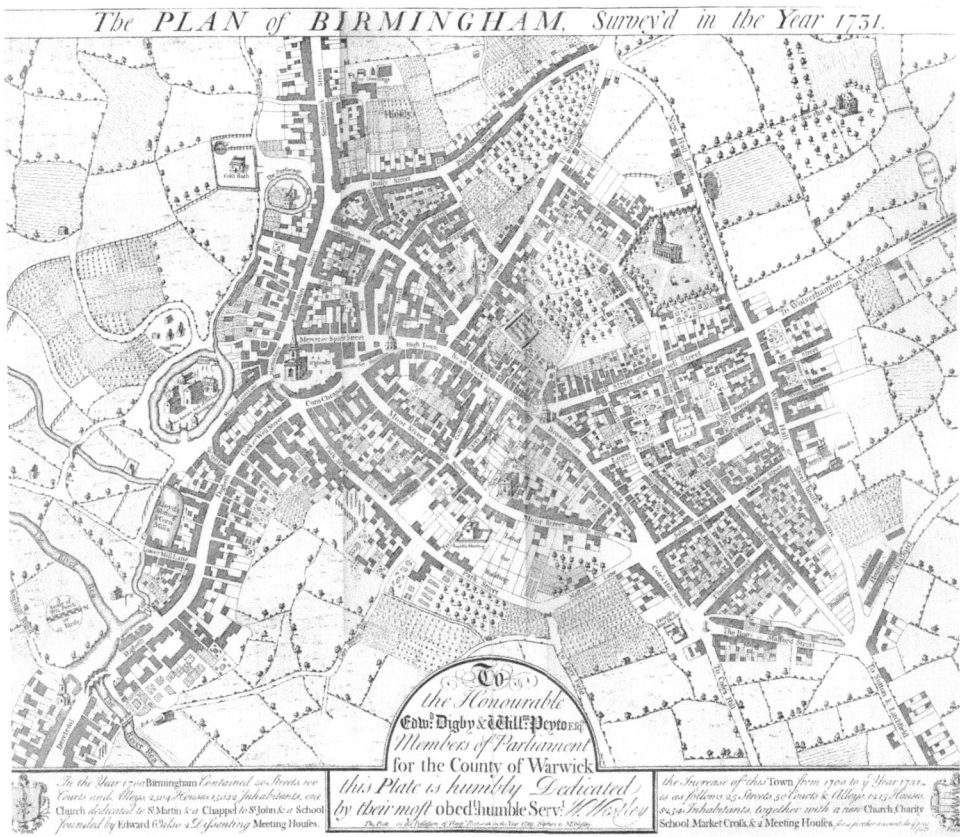

Westley's Plan of Birmingham *in 1731 showing the original Steelhouse almshouses as two shaded lines on the bottom right above the junction of five streets.*

Shown on the first map of Birmingham in 1731, the Steelhouse Lane almshouses were also cleared for building leases and replaced nearby by a new building with 42 apartments. They bore the inscription, "These almshouses built by the Trustees of Lench's Trust, in the year 1764. W. Walsingham, Bailiff". Costing £320, another three rooms were added in 1814. Their residents became the first in the locality to benefit from the new form of lighting with gas from the burning of coal. In 1830, through the solicitation of the Bailiff of Lench's Trust, Thomas Ryland, the Birmingham Gas Light Company "very generously agreed to light a lamp *gratuitously* in court-yard". The gesture was praised as bringing great comfort to the poor women inhabiting the dwellings. Ageing as they were, in 1880 the Steelhouse Lane almshouses were sold for £10,000 to the council to be cleared for its Improvement Scheme. (*Aris's Birmingham Gazette*, 18 June 1764 and *Birmingham Journal*, 22 May 1830).

The second set of Steelhouse Lane almshouses shortly before they were cleared in the early 1880s.

Nineteenth-Century Almshouse Expansion

The almshouse provision by Lench's was increased in 1801 with the building of a set of 32 in Dudley Street. They cost £539, although £120 was defrayed by selling old material on the site. Fourteen years later, 16 almshouses were built in Park Street on part of the Moor Street Estate. The outlay was £794, including £40 for the lease of the house which had stood on the site. Sixteen more houses were added in 1820 for £633. The funds were raised via loans to supplement "the accumulations in hand". This borrowed money was repaid by 1827, when the Trust had £121 in cash and £500 in the bank.

That year, land was bought in Hospital Street for building more almshouses. This purchase was partly enabled by the money raised in the previous century from the sale of Wrixham's property in Spiceal Street for the expansion of St. Martin's Churchyard. In 1829 the project was completed. There were 34 rooms built in blocks of a quadrangle with the Matron's House adjoining the street. One block was named 'Mansells Houses' as it was paid for by legacies of £100 each from Mrs. Judith Mansell, Mrs. Mary Mansell, and Mrs. Sarah Mansell.

The bleaker Hospital Street almshouses in the midst of a poor and industrial district.

The Lord Mayor, Alderman Perceval Bower OBE JP arriving with the Trustees at the Hospital Street almshouses as part of the celebrations for Lench's 400th anniversary in 1925. On the left is a large electro-plating works.

Musgrove made an interesting point about these almshouses. Though unattractive in both their setting and appearance, it was curious that "the inmates of these houses live longer and suffer less illness than at any other of the almshouses, in spite of the fact that the rooms … are smaller, are surrounded by factories, and close to the Electrical Generating Station of the Corporation". Writing in the early 1920s, he found it difficult to explain this but stressed that the records for the previous 20 years proved it without a doubt. He also commented that the Trustees were installing electric lights so that "the lives of the inmates may be brightened during the winter evenings at any rate".

As part of the plans for New Street Station, in 1848, the Dudley Street almshouses were bought by the London and North-Western Railway. Along with the money from the sale of properties in Moor Street, that purchase funded the building of the Ravenhurst Street almshouses at Camp Hill at a cost of almost £6,000, plus £500 for the land. Originally, the Trustees looked at a site they owned in Woodcock Street but abandoned that idea to buy a plot on Singer's Hill. That, too, was not taken forward and instead the land was leased to the Birmingham Hebrew congregation, who built the magnificent Grade II* Singer's Hill Synagogue there.

The magnificent Singer's Hill Synagogue built on Lench's land.

The Ravenhurst Street almshouses with a grass courtyard, trees and bushes – all absent from Hospital Street.

The 48 rooms at Ravenhurst Street weren't ready until 1849 and before moving in, the residents from the Dudley Street almshouses stayed at Bingley House for a short time. Formerly the home of one of the banking Lloyds, it would soon be knocked down for Bingley Hall – now the site of the ICC.

Though laid out on similar lines to those in Hospital Street, the Jacobean-style Ravenhurst Street almshouses were more attractive and much pleasanter, surrounded as they were with private houses and having a lawn and flower beds in the quadrangle. They were followed in 1859 by the Ladywood Road almshouses, also opened with the same number of rooms and to the same plan other than a glass verandah along the whole front. Replacing the Park Street almshouses, the new facility cost £5,013 and £1,200 for the land, with the money raised by selling various properties to railway companies and by the falling in of leases.

The building went ahead even though the Charity Commissioners made strong objections, preferring as they did a policy of pension schemes to almshouses. Their objections didn't deter the Trustees' belief in the importance of new almshouses, as made plain in the Bailiff's Report of 1868.

I notice that in each annual report for several years past the Bailiff for the time being has reminded the Trustees of the pressing want of additional almshouses and I can truly say from my year's experience as Bailiff the want still continues and is increasing.

There are at present more than 100 applicants on the books, many have been waiting for years, and are eligible cases. I cannot doubt that another set of houses is urgently needed, and if any benevolent individual contemplating the endowment of almshouses could be prevailed upon to lend a helping hand towards the erection of a new set of houses in connection with the Charity I am sure a great boon would be conferred upon the town. I am reminded by the solicitor that such helping hands have in former times been extended to this Trust, and that in fact the Trust property is but a collection under the name of Lench's trust of gifts by various charitable persons. The names of Colmore, Vesey, Wrixham, Kilcuppe, Shelton, Ward, Mansell, and Scott will be remembered with gratitude for years to some as Founders in this excellent Charity, the benefits of which can be conferred in the most simple and expedient manner and without any of those disturbing influences which sometimes beset Charities where Religious, Educational, or Political differences of opinion arise or are allowed to prevail.

It would be 12 years before a new set of almshouses were opened, and then they were not an addition but a replacement for those in Steelhouse Lane. Like the earlier buildings, the Conybere Street almshouses of 1880 were divided into blocks

The frontage of the Ladywood almshouses to the left of the Children's Hospital on the right.

The Ladywood almshouses.

of four rooms, half on the ground floor and half above. By contrast, though, they had several larger blocks, whilst the whole building was more ambitious in scale. Its 48 rooms were set around three sides of a quadrangle with the matron's house in the middle of the open end facing the street. Within the quadrangle was another block intended as an infirmary. Unfortunately, none of the residents used it and the rooms remained empty until 1911, when seven of them were given over to almswomen and the eighth became a meeting room.

Standing next to the Grade II* listed church of St. Alban's, the Conybere Street almshouses were also distinguished architecturally and are themselves Grade II listed. Designed by the celebrated J. A. Chatwin, they were the first example of the 'Queen Anne' style in Birmingham. Noticeably, they featured late seventeenth-century detailing in moulded and cut brickwork on the pilasters, string courses, and eaves of the façades nearest to the street. The building was further distinguished by tall star-shaped chimneys.

Elegant in design as it was, the almshouse project was expensive to build and upkeep. Just over £1,800 was paid for the land, whilst the considerable sum of £12,290 was spent on construction – much more than was estimated. The compulsory purchase of the Steelhouse Lane almshouses by the council for its Improvement Scheme brought in £10,000 and another £1,000 came from a bequest from the Reverend Clement Ingleby. Though praised architecturally,

The frontage of the Conybere Street almshouses, a striking building in a poor neighbourhood packed with back-to-backs and factories.

Musgrove was critical of the new building. Doubtful as to whether the large expenditure was justified, he emphasised that the red sandstone of the ornamental façade, as with other public buildings, wouldn't stand Birmingham's polluted air. With a good deal of money spent in attempts at restoring the stone, he believed it was quite possible that the façade would have to come down. Thankfully, it hasn't.

Two residents looking down from a window at the Lord Mayor, Alderman Perceval Bower OBE JP (left) with Arthur Musgrove, clerk (right), and Bailiff Frederick Buck Goodman (behind) at the Conybere Street almshouses in 1925.

Chapter 9

Ladies' Committee, Matrons, and Residents

The Ladies' Committee

Various criteria were adopted to choose successful applicants for the almshouses. Before 1789, each Trustee had a nomination until it was decided that an election for applicants would take place at a general meeting of all the Trustees. Thereafter, the Senior Bailiff had the sole power of appointment. With Birmingham's population rising so quickly, the number of applicants increased substantially and in 1868, Dr. James Russell senior, a Unitarian involved in other good causes to help the poor, reported that he'd assessed 134 people in his year of office. As this was too onerous a responsibility, he suggested that another method of enquiring into characters was needed to enable a better selection.

The last almsman was appointed in 1780 and from 1821, the Trustees decided that only aged women were eligible. Still, no women were involved in any way in Trust decisions until Russell's suggestion was acted upon by his successor. Another Unitarian and large-scale metal manufacturer, Charles Clifford asked two unknown female members of his family to visit candidates in their home. The next year, 1879, each Trustee was asked to depute a woman from his family to assist in the work of assessment. Six responded. Again, their names weren't recorded but they interviewed the candidates and supervised the almshouses.

Though thanked annually for their services, the women remained anonymous and acted within the constraints of the Victorian patriarchy. As one Bailiff explained, they were his 'Privy Council', but whilst they greatly lessened his anxiety and labour, they were "careful not to interfere with his authority or privileges". However, in 1882 the Charity Commissioners' Scheme included provision for the properly constituted involvement of women.

> For the purpose of assisting the Bailiffs and Trustees in the selection of Almswomen and in the general visitation of the almshouses and their inmates, the Trustees shall be at liberty to appoint a Visiting Committee

consisting of no more than nine women, who shall, subject to the direction of the Bailiffs, assist them in the performance of those duties, and of any other duties of visitation and control which may be assigned to them.

Upper middle-class women were increasingly involved in social work, thanks mainly to the efforts of Octavia Hill. A highly influential woman passionate about social and housing reform, in 1864 she persuaded her friend and mentor John Ruskin, the art and social critic, to invest in her dream of improving the housing for "my friends among the poor" to make "lives noble, homes happy, and family life good". Hill's material, moral and social considerations were underpinned by a highly personal approach to dealing with the tenants in the properties she oversaw. This was achieved through weekly visits by educated, single middle-class women to collect the rent. They checked on the premises and through developing personal contacts with wives and children especially, they forged personal bonds between the classes. These female rent collectors were the precursors of professional women housing and social workers.

The Lord Mayor, Alderman Perceval Bower OBE JP speaking with Mrs. Fisher at the Ravenhurst Street almshouses during the celebrations of Lench's 400th anniversary in 1925. Behind him is the Clerk, Arthur Musgrove, and with her back to the camera is Mrs. Padmore, 'chairman' of the Ladies' Committee.

Unlike the single women working with Hill and other pioneering housing associations, Lench's Ladies' Committee, as it was better known, involved married women. One of the first was Ellen Smith, née Osler, a Unitarian like her husband, Howard Samuel Smith, the chartered accountant responsible for Lench's accounts. Mostly as secretary, she served on the Committee for over 30 years until her death in 1914 when she was succeeded by her niece Muriel Worsley, née Smith.

Other prominent women included Margaret Lilla Martineau, a Kenrick by birth and the wife and mother of lord mayors of Birmingham, and Ursula Burman, née Hesketh-Wright from a well-known Edgbaston family. Her husband, John Charles Burman, became Birmingham's youngest lord mayor in 1947 and she herself was committed to public service. During the Second World War, she nursed at the Accident Hospital,

Lady Ursula Burman, wife of Sir Charles Burman, knighted in 1961 for his political and industrial career.
(Birmingham Mail, 5 October 2012; thanks to the Birmingham Mail).

was a member of both the St. John Ambulance Brigade and the Civil Nursing Reserve and was also a group organiser of the Women's Volunteer Housewives' Section. With the coming of peace, and in addition to her responsibilities as the mother of four children, she was on the council of the Church of England College and the Board of Birmingham's United Hospitals and was a member of the Nursing Committee. (*Birmingham Daily Gazette*, 30 July 1947).

Devised over time by the Ladies' Committee, the system of selection and admission for applicants involved an exhaustive procedure of several stages. A register was kept but was opened only at intervals, sometimes for several years. This event was advertised widely in Birmingham's newspapers, with applicants having to fill in a prescribed form handed in to a matron and then checked by the Clerk at an interview in their homes. Those who passed his inspection were in turn interviewed by the Ladies' Committee, who selected the most suitable candidates. Their list was submitted to the Trustees for approval and when granted, the selected names were entered on the register which was then closed. More interviews followed at meetings of the Ladies' Committee and when a vacancy arose, they chose a name for approval by the Bailiff. Demand was high and in 1923 there were 264 applications with 174 of them finally approved. With the number of vacancies averaging between 18 and 20 a year it would be almost 10 years before the register was reopened.

The Lord Mayor, Alderman Perceval Bower OBE JP speaking with Mrs. Jones, Mrs. Bannister, and Mrs. Brown at the Ravenhurst Street almshouses when celebrating Lench's 400th anniversary in 1925.

Though realising that the system was somewhat elaborate, Musgrove was certain that it was as near perfect as possible "for any system to be for choosing the most deserving or urgent applicant out of a large number of deserving cases". The crucial word here was 'deserving'. Although it was "absolutely unsectarian in its operations" and asked no questions about the religion of applicants, still the Trustees, Clerk, and members of the Ladies' Committee were imbued with class-biased notions dividing the poor into those who deserved help and those who didn't. The 'deserving' were those deemed respectable according to middle-class attitudes. Clean, moderate in their habits, thrifty, and respectful to their 'betters', they were needy because of circumstances outside their control, such as disability, age, sickness, widowhood, or injury. The 'undeserving' were those who didn't conform to those standards and who were viewed as culpable in their poverty through their own faults and actions.

Such a harsh and discriminatory approach was legalised through the Poor Law Amendment Act of 1834. Its objective was to punish the 'undeserving' for asking for help by forcing them into hated workhouses where they lost all freedom and dignity. Once inside they became paupers with few rights, as did those who asked for temporary relief outside the workhouse. Both those receiving indoor and outdoor relief were overseen by the Board of Guardians, all of whom were male property owners. In 1850 they decided to reduce the allowance of paupers in Lench's almshouse by sixpence a week as they desired that such accommodation should be "a sort of reward for poor but independent persons". In response, Lench's solicitor, Thomas Eyre Lee, wrote that the Trustees "were anxious to carry out these views; and it was their intention not to afford the benefits of the almshouses to paupers in future. For the present, however, they requested that those inmates who had been paupers should be allowed the same amount as formerly". That was agreed. (*Aris's Birmingham Gazette*, 4 November 1850).

The Ladies' Committee did not challenge the class-prejudiced assessment of 'inmates', a term which itself was imbued with discrimination used as it was for prisoners and those forced to go into the workhouse. From 1850, women over 60 who were accepted had to fulfil several requirements. Widows or spinsters of good character, honest, sober, and cleanly, they must have resided in Birmingham for at least five years. During that period, they should not have received Poor Law Relief nor been "unable to manage themselves without their own exertions" because of age, ill-health, accident, or infirmity.

They also needed to have an income of 5 shillings a week in their own right or be guaranteed that sum by three relatives or friends – although the former had precedence. Finally, there was "a preference for those persons, who, being otherwise qualified as aforesaid, shall have become reduced by misfortune from better circumstances". Enquiries were made as to the character, antecedents, and means of the applicants and of the means of any guarantors. False statements or misrepresentation disqualified an applicant whilst those in an almshouse would forfeit their place. Despite this, cases of non-payment of the guaranteed income were mostly not reported, and if they were, action was very difficult to enforce. (*Birmingham Daily Mail*, 25 May 1891).

Matrons

Each set of almshouses was overseen by a matron living in a lodge on site, although the Bailiff visited the rooms once a quarter. Responsible for looking after the residents, she was also entrusted with ensuring that they kept the rules; maintained their rooms cleanliness; did not stay out after 10pm at night; and applied for the Bailiff's permission if they wanted to go away for more than a day. There is no indication of who actually supervised the residents until Mrs. Ann Starling, née Rossiter, was appointed in 1839. Her background indicated that she was not from the poor.

Born in Shepton Mallet, Somerset in 1788, as a young teenager she moved to London to join her older sister in service with Lady Vincent before becoming maid to Lady Walpole. Her 10 years' employment "was nothing but one long round of late hours and enervating gaiety; for my lady was a famous Court beauty and leader of fashion, whose dresses cost £500 apiece, who gave grand parties, and visited everywhere. Mrs. Starling frequently had to dress her mistress for two or three balls and receptions of a night. When Lady Walpole gave a dance, her maid presided at the ice and refreshment tables till long after chanticleer (cockrell) proclaimed the morn". Still the grandest scene she ever saw, one she never forgot, was at the Duke of Devonshire's in Piccadilly when the Tsar of Russia, the King of Prussia, and Field-Marshal Blücher were entertained at a magnificent fête. Amongst Mrs. Starling's other reminiscences were the first gas-lighting she saw, "And how it did surprise us all, after being so used to the old oil lamps. We thought wonders would never cease".

Engaged to a tradesman's son, Lady Walpole bought Ann Starling's wedding dress and furnished a house for the couple, even to the silver. Sadly, her fiancé died of consumption a few days before their wedding. Happily, after a few years, she fell in love again and married, moving with her husband to Birmingham where he worked for the Mining Copper Company. Following his death after a works' injury, Ann Starling was left with children to support and "but for the kindness of one of the firm she might have found herself in necessitous circumstances. It was through his instrumentality that she was appointed matron of one of the lodges of Lench's Trust. So much satisfaction did she give that she was afterwards entrusted with the supervision of all the almshouses under the Trust".

First serving as matron of the Hospital Street almshouses, Ann Starling's two young sons lived with her. She then went on to the Ladywood almshouses, retiring in her 70s. After a time with one of her family, she travelled to America to visit a son. She was 84 and stayed there for two years. Returning to Birmingham, she rented a house in Ladywood and took in a boarder, before moving back into the local almshouses. A local newspaper reported that:

> … if she had her choice of the whole town she could not have a more congenial habitation … where every want is studied by a kind matron and the nurse who never leaves her, and where smiling faces gather round, and chase away the gloom from the long winter of an eventful life. How many people of half her age are heard to say that the dregs of life are not worth

having. These querulous pessimists should visit Ladywood, if they wish to see an edifying picture of old age and perfect contentment.

On Ann Starling's 100th birthday, there were 'high jinks' and "she sat in state all day receiving visitors, chatted gaily to numerous Edgbaston ladies who drove up in their carriages with congratulatory birthday cards, and told the long story of her life a dozen times over without showing the slightest symptom of fatigue". Boasting that she never had an ailment in her life or needed a walking stick, she stressed that she didn't like to lie in bed late like an old woman. One of her rules was "to make sure and have a good meat dinner whatever happens". Although abstemious, she wasn't an abstainer, and enjoyed stout and sherry in moderation, but had a strong dislike to spirits, with nothing disgusting her so much as gin drinking among women. In 1891 aged 103, she died quietly in her sleep but was praised as instigating "many of the improvements which have made Lench's Trust the model institution it is today". (*Birmingham Daily Mail*, 16 April 1888, *Weston Mercury,* 3 October 1891, and Censuses).

The Lord Mayor, Alderman Perceval Bower OBE JP with Mrs. Piper, the oldest almswoman, at the Ladywood Road almshouses as part of the celebrations for Lench's 400th anniversary in 1925.

Residents

By then, matrons received 15 shillings a week, up from 10 shillings since 1841, with the coal and gas for their house paid by the Trust. They had a feather bed whilst the residents' rooms were fitted out with metal bedsteads, hair mattresses, oak corner cupboards and chests of drawers, deal tables, windsor chairs, fenders, grates, fire irons, blind rollers, and gas pipes. Almswomen were allowed to bring in their own furniture provided it didn't overcrowd their room. Outside, they had the use of a washhouse, water butts, line props, and washing and other tubs. From 1801, they were supplied with an allowance of coal, increasing to 100 weight a week from 1872, with more in cold weather. This was a much needed and expensive gesture from the Trust, as coal was the main fuel for warmth and for heating the black-leaded ranges for cooking. Another unusual and important benefit in an era when the poor couldn't afford doctors was the provision of medical attendance during illness. (*Birmingham Daily Gazette*, 28 April 1879 and *Aris's Birmingham Gazette*, 21 August 1880).

Despite the restrictive admission criteria, the benefits of an almshouse were considerable. Birmingham's poor lived in badly built, insanitary back-to-backs injurious to health. Costing 3s 6d a week, they were beyond the reach of an aged single woman with a weekly income as low as 5 shillings, when the poverty line was put at about £1 a week. In such circumstances, either they took in lodgers, carried on working with increasing difficulty in laborious and dirty jobs, moved in with relatives, or went to the workhouse.

Lench's provided a more favourable option if admission were achieved, whilst the benefits of private rooms were enhanced by the distribution of the Trust's surplus income to almswomen. With the running down of the practice of including the poor of Birmingham generally, in 1783 residents were given a stipend of 1s a week. Twice a year at Christmas and Easter, this was supplemented with gifts of money fixed in 1789 at 5 shillings. This was increased to 10 shillings at Christmas and 5 shillings on three other occasions a year following the gift of Mrs. Ann Scott.

In 1808 and 1809 she gave the Trustees a total of £630, which was used to buy property in Upper Priory. As a party to the conveyance, Mrs. Scott directed that the income be distributed equally to the residents of the almshouses. In 1868, the building was leased to the Children's Hospital and knocked down for a new Outpatients Department. Lench's charged the low annual rent of £100 for 99 years for the land, favourable terms obtained thanks to John D. Goodman, a Trustee as well as a committee member of the Children's Hospital. A leading merchant and gun manufacturer, he was involved in many good causes. The site was purchased by the hospital in 1892.

The quarterly payments were ended in 1858 and replaced by a fixed weekly stipend of 2 shillings 6 pence, gradually increasing to 4 shillings from 1879. This was one of the many privileges extolled in an article in the *Birmingham Daily Gazette* in 1905. The reporter stressed that those fortunate to gain admission as a tenant under Lench's Charity had finished their struggle for existence and were gently lulled in the security of a placid backwater. Subject to observing the rules, their benefits included a gift that was almost priceless – peace. The Conybere Street almshouses were taken as an example.

> It spells tranquility.
>
> Graceful arcading shuts it off from the rude gaze of the street, while westwards, the cathedral-like walls of St. Albans Church tower above it, as a protecting turret. A cat or two prowl about the precincts, but the butcher's lad and the baker's-boy instinctively retrain their desire to desecrate the hostel with their whistling. The milkman, like a man who knows his duty to age, sinks his voice to a murmur – unless the almswoman is deaf. And so the lives of the old ladies spend themselves slowly and quietly away, and, in due course, make room for some of those applicants who to-day knock upon the matron's door. (*Evening Despatch*, 29 April 1905).

The Lord Mayor, Alderman Perceval Bower OBE JP with Miss Hill, Miss Bartlam and other almswomen at the Ladywood Road almshouses as part of the celebrations for Lench's 400th anniversary in 1925. Trustees and members of the Ladies' Committee are also in the photograph.

Who were these women? In language that we today would see as demeaning to women, the reporter described the applicants as respectably poor, but in appearance as diverse as the flowers in the field. Some were "plump and comfortable, others spare and shrewish; some stylish in hats, others subdued – and sometimes frumpish – in bonnets; some bustling and domineering, others decrepit and tottering dependent".

Unfortunately, there is little evidence regarding individual almswomen other than the name recorded in decennial censuses. However, a few of these which also recorded their former occupations are instructive as they indicate a clear bias in the Trust accepting women who fitted into the dominant middle-class attitudes of what was regarded as womanly. Birmingham's manufacturers depended greatly on female workers, either in factories and workshops or as outworkers in their homes. Such occupations were frowned upon as too masculine. Button making, in particular, employed many women, yet out of the 47 residents in the Ravenhurst Street almshouses in 1851, only three had worked in that trade. Indeed, they were the only ones who'd been involved in industry, although several occupations are illegible.

Poor mothers with large families had to take on the worst paid jobs of all, cleaning the homes of the better-off and washing their clothes in washhouses in the shared yards of back-to-backs. Both were arduous and heavy tasks, as was

The dreadful working conditions of washerwomen in a back-to-back yard in Florence Street, off Holloway Head, in 1933. The older woman stands in front of a mangle, often owned by a woman who hired it out. To the right, the maiding tubs are the larger part of beer barrels, in which women pounded clean the washing with a maid, a long, thick piece of wood with a block of wood at the bottom. On top of one of them is the swilling tub, the smaller part of the beer barrel. Behind them is a mother and her child in the communal brew'us, washhouse, where washing would be boiled in a copper set in brick and under which a fire was lit. The brew'us has no door or window and is covered only by corrugated iron. Taking in the clothes of the middle class, washer women worked whatever the weather.

mangling, pressing water out of washed clothes between two heavy, smooth, round bars. Yet the census noted only seven washerwomen, charwomen, and keepers of mangles. By contrast, the great majority of the residents were involved in what were regarded as socially acceptable and respectable female occupations. There were nurses, servants, and needlewomen, as well as a cook, sempstress, and bonnet maker. Women from lower middle-class backgrounds also featured, including two housekeepers, a governess, school mistress, and collector of rents.

The 1861 Census for the Steelhouse Lane almshouses made it clear that women from the most poor or industrial backgrounds were least favoured by the Trust. Again, with the proviso that not all occupations were legible, out of 42 residents merely six were washerwomen or charwomen; and even though the building stood amid Birmingham's Gun Quarter, just one woman had worked in that trade with another five having been involved in manufacturing. Two more had been warehouse women, regarded as clean work acceptable for single women. Most of the residents reflected those at Ravenhurst Street 10 years before, again with a smattering of those from the lower middle class.

Ranging from 61-years old to 96, 22 women were in their 70s and seven in their 80s and 90s. These were remarkable ages when the death rates amongst poor people were appallingly high, and few could expect to live into their 60s.

The Lord Mayor, Alderman Perceval Bower OBE JP with a group of almswomen at the Ravenhurst Street almshouses during the celebrations for Lench's 400th anniversary in 1925. They are Mrs. Whitehouse, Mrs. Fisher, Mrs. Robinson, Mrs. Parkes, Mrs. Taunton, Mrs. Johnson, Mrs. Young, Mrs. Argent, Mrs. Naylor, and Mrs. Silman.

Such longevity can be explained not only by the good facilities provided by Lench's but also by the backgrounds of so many of the women. Whilst servants and others in 'female' occupations may not have been paid well, they'd lived and worked in better conditions than the likes of washerwomen and those in manufacturing.

One of the Steelhouse Lane residents was a baker born in France, but although there were a few from elsewhere in England, most were from Birmingham and nearby districts, with a smattering from the Welsh borders. One of the local women was Mary Cullen. Formerly an upholsteress, 20 years before, she was a widow supplementing her income by taking in a family of four to her small home in the poor quarter of Bartholomew Street. She then moved into the almshouses but in 1862 died tragically. Having heard faint groans from her room, Ann Lee, who lived opposite, went in and raised the alarm when seeing 85-year-old Mary Cullen enveloped in flames. The matron ran inside with a blanket and "with the assistance of two gentlemen who were passing at the time, succeeded in extinguishing the flames". By then unhappily, Mrs. Cullen "was quite dead". (*Aris's Birmingham Gazette*, 4 January 1862).

A rare death notice like this gave a fleeting glimpse of life before the almshouse. In 1864, 69-year-old Sarah Jones died from an accident. One January morning she left home, with the permission of the matron, to see some friends. Soon after, the matron was sent to the General Hospital where Sarah Jones was lying with a fractured left leg. She explained that she'd been crossing the 'horse-road' and endeavouring to get out of the way of a horse and cab, she was knocked over by a horse drawing a cartload of hay. One of the wheels then went over her leg. The horses were going at a slow pace, and Sarah Jones didn't blame anyone.

Unhappily, although properly attended to at the hospital, she gradually sank and died. A charwoman from Monmouthshire in South Wales, she'd lived with her husband in Gloucester before moving to Birmingham in the 1850s. (*Birmingham Daily Gazette*, 13 January 1864).

In 1875, 78-year-old Mary Bowater was another unusual resident at Lench's in dying in tragic circumstances. Born in Chester, when but a teenager, she married a soldier. He fought at Waterloo in 1815, with her close at hand. By 1841, she was widowed and living with her three sons and two daughters. The youngest was four and the oldest 15 and he and two others were working. Ten years later, Mary Bowater was renting a back-to-back in Duke Street, one of the poorest parts of Birmingham where Lench's owned property as part of the Woodcock Croft Estate. Still named as the head of the household, her son, his wife, and their two children lived with her. So did her youngest daughter and a female lodger. Things were very cramped and it's likely that her son and his family slept in one bedroom and the three other women in the second.

After such overcrowding, Mary Bowater must have welcomed a room to herself at the Steelhouse Lane almshouses. Unfortunately, though, one night she sat too near to her fire, and her clothes were set alight. Alerted by her shouts, another resident ran to her but found her enveloped in flames. Smoke filled her room and the linen on the fire guard was burning. With the flames spreading to the furniture, water was thrown over Mary Bowater but, burned badly over all parts of her body, she died in the nearby General Hospital – built on land formerly owned by Lench's. It must be borne in mind that in a period when heating came from open fires over which cooking was done, that sadly, deaths by burning or scalding were commonplace. (*Birmingham Mail*, 17 July 1875).

Sir John Smedley Crooke, Conservative MP for Deritend, with Mrs. Randall and Mrs. Brown and other almswomen at the Ravenhurst almshouses as part of the celebrations for Lench's 400th anniversary in 1925.

Chapter 10

Into the Twentieth Century

The 1915 Scheme: Trustees

In his history of the Trust, Arthur Musgrove made it clear that the turn of the twentieth century was a landmark for Lench's. He was right. Its income rose dramatically from about £650 in 1849 to upwards of £3,000 in 1886 and £4,197 in 1898. Stipends to almswomen took out £1,829; the salaries of matrons and payments for coal, water, gas, and incidentals totalled £958; estate repairs, insurances, and taxes cost £789; the clerk's salary, the rent of the office, fees for auditors, solicitors, surveyors and rent collectors, and the purchase of stationery and printing amounted to £383; and the bank charges and interest were £117. That left a surplus of just £128.

Ten years later, the Trust's finances received a significant boost from the sale of vacant land between Moor Street and Park Street to the Great Western Railway for the big sum of £20,000. This was followed in 1909 by selling the greater part of the Callowfields Estate to the Council for £5,000. Flush with money, Lench's was able to wipe out both its usual deficiency between income and expenditure and its bank overdraft. This healthy financial state allowed the Trustees to apply to the Charity Commission for a scheme to create pensions for its almswomen. (*Birmingham Mail,* 15 February 1886 and *Birmingham Daily Post,* 14 February 1898).

After much correspondence and negotiation, on 17 May 1915, the Commissioners made an amending scheme, which included reorganising the constitution of the Trustees in a more democratic manner. It's interesting that this occurred in the second year of the First World War when all classes in the country were urged to unite to work and fight for victory. Under the amendment, the property rate qualification for Trustees was abolished along with the necessity of the approval of the Commissioners for their appointment. Henceforth, Trustees had to be 16 competent persons, eight Representative and eight Co-optative.

The four existing Representatives were to hold office for life but the four new ones and all those to follow were appointed for a term of three years by the council. These Trustees didn't have to be councillors or residents of Birmingham. Unlike

Inside the entrance at the Ravenhurst Street almshouses in 1925 as part of the celebrations for Lench's 400th anniversary in 1925. On the left is Trustee Wilfrid Byng Kenrick, and next to him is the Surveyor of Lench's, Ernest Lakin Smith. To the right of the tree is Bailiff Frederick Buck Goodman and next to him with his back to the camera is the Lord Mayor, Alderman Perceval Bower OBE JP. The man sitting beside him is Trustee Sir David Davis in conversation with Sir John Smedley Crooke MP. Behind the pillar is Henry Lloyd Wilson, the Junior Bailiff, and to the right are Trustee Boultbee Brookes and Clerk Arthur Musgrove.

them, Co-optative Trustees had to live in the city or carry on a business there or nearby. Seven of the positions were given for life to the existing Elective Trustees, but new members were to be appointed for five years by resolution of the Trustees. That seven included some familiar names in Ernest Martineau, Hubert Kenrick Beale, and Wilfred Byng Kenrick. Within five years, they were joined by the first female Trustee, Miss Adelaide Jane Lloyd. One of the Quaker banking family, her own father was a large-scale ironmaster in Wednesbury.

The second Lady Superintendent of the Children's Hospital, she operated as the matron whilst she was also responsible for the training of the nurses. Elected in 1919 as a Conservative and Unionist, she was also a pioneering woman on Birmingham Council. Standing for re-election two years later, she emphasised that it was "important that a great effort should be made to retain this Seat for a Woman. The City Council consists of 120 Members, of whom only 7 are Women". She lost to the Labour candidate.

In 1925, a second female Trustee was appointed. She was Mrs. Theodora Mary Wilson. Two years previously and standing as Mrs. Henry Lloyd Wilson, she was elected a Labour councillor for Selly Oak. A local Quaker and peace activist, she maintained that at least one out of the three councillors in every ward should be a woman. In particular, and although she was middle class, she felt that she could represent working-class mothers because "I have lived in close touch with my fellow women citizens … and know the appalling conditions under which many of them live". A councillor until 1932, she became chair of the Maternity and Child Welfare Committee and was involved in the Housing Committee.

Municipal Election, 1923.
POLLING DAY——THURSDAY, NOV. 1st.

Mrs. HENRY LLOYD WILSON
The Labour Candidate.

Appointed in 1925, Mrs. Theodora Mary Wilson was the second female Trustee and a pioneering woman councillor in Birmingham. (Library of Birmingham).

The 1915 Scheme: Pensions

The 1915 Scheme also stated that any residue of income should be applied in pensions for women not living in almshouses but with the same qualifications as those that did. This amount was to be no less than 4 shillings and no more than 10 shillings. In implementing this requirement, the Trustees decided to grant pensions to three types of women. The first were those residents affected by 'mental infirmity', ill health or other causes who could no longer look after themselves and would be more comfortably looked after in the homes of relatives or friends. This was the most successful and useful part of the Pension Scheme. The second class were women on the selected list for almshouses but waiting for admission. At first, 40 of them were supported but their numbers dropped rapidly, and by 1923 only one remained. That year there were no surplus funds, and no other such pensions were granted.

The third group was "women of a superior class to the average Almswomen for whom a pension would be more suitable than an Almshouse". Still influenced by class distinctions, the Trust identified these women as having been reduced by misfortune from better circumstances. Twelve women were quickly identified from the list of those selected for admission, with another 20 'excellent candidates' found from enquiries made to other local charities. By 1923, 27 pensioners belonged to this more privileged group compared with the 19 who'd been sent away to relatives, although not by any compulsion.

In 1921, a short additional scheme raised the maximum weekly payments for almswomen to 10 shillings 6 pence and for the 47 outside pensioners to 15 shillings. Musgrove concluded that almshouses built at a moderate cost were the best mode of relieving distress, although pensions were most suitable for some women in the same circumstances as almswomen. He also pointed out that the lives of women aged 70 and over were improved by the Old Age Pension Act of 1908. Originally it provided 5 shillings a week for those eligible. A means-tested benefit, the full amount was paid to those with incomes below £21 a year, with a sliding scale of reductions for those bringing in between £21 and £31 10 shillings annually. The Trustees ensured that those almswomen who qualified received their state pension along with their weekly stipend, increased to 8 shillings from 1911. A decade later, and because of the increase in the cost of living after the First World War, the Trustees announced that residents under 70 would receive a weekly payment of 10 shillings 6 pence.

The Lord Mayor, Alderman Perceval Bower OBE JP with almswomen at the Ravenhurst Street almshouses as part of the celebrations for Lench's 400th anniversary in 1925. They were beneficiaries of the 1908 Old Age Pension Act.

Residents

It wasn't until the mid-1930s that one of the residents of Lench's came more clearly into view. She was 82-year-old Maria Ball, née Atkins. Her Irish father, William, moved to Birmingham before the Great Hunger, the famine that ravaged Ireland. Starting off as a labourer, he went on to gain skills as a brewer, making a living working for some of the many home-brewed pubs in Birmingham in the 1860s. He and his wife, Hannah, from Handsworth, raised a big family in and around the Jewellery Quarter, with Maria one of the youngest. After her father died, she and several other children still lived with their widowed mother, with Maria working as a gold chain maker. She didn't marry until 1904, at the late age of 48 for a working-class woman, and was nine years older than her husband, William Ball, a porter. By 1921, though, she was widowed and scraping a living as a charwoman. Having no family of her own, she was lodging with another widow and her son.

Maria's life must have improved when she moved into Lench's and drew their stipend along with her old age pension. Indeed, she was able to take an annual holiday in Blackpool, not picking out the sedate attractions but exploring "all the happy and exciting entertainments – especially the thrills of the Pleasure Beach". In 1935, her thrill was her first flight.

Dubbed by the local press as a 'Merry Widow', she said that "Flying is lovely". It was one of her two big desires. The other was to live to 100. Unhappily, she

Three oldest members of the Lench Trust party of almswomen, which left Birmingham for Trentham Gardens to-day. They are Mrs. Hopkins, Mrs. Jackson, and Mrs. Almond, all aged 87, and they are seen talking to the organisers, Mr. A. Musgrove (secretary to the trustees) and Mr. G. E. Allen (right).

Evening Despatch, 9 June 1937. (Thanks to the Birmingham Mail).

failed to do that by 11 years, dying in 1945. (*Birmingham Weekly Mercury*, 21 July 1935).

Two years after Maria Ball was featured, the three oldest residents in Lench's appeared in a photograph in the *Evening Despatch*. They were about to set out on a day trip to Trentham Gardens organised by Arthur Musgrove to celebrate the Coronation of George VI. The trio were Mrs. Sarah Jackson, Mrs. Hopkins, and Mrs. Almond, all aged 87. The article accompanying them focused on an 85-year-old called Martha bedecked with a wreath of flowers around her hat. The other 152 excursionists were as resplendent and New Street "on the day of Queen Victoria's Jubilee could not have presented a finer garden display than this sea of hats decorated with roses, poppies, daisies, violets, and other floral creations, with the colour of one flower and the shape of the other".

When asked if she was going to sit in the gardens and enjoy the sunshine, Martha replied:

> No, bless you. We're out for a bit of fun. If I don't go on the swings today, I might be too old for it next year!
>
> Last year there was three of us got playing that clock golf – and having that much fun we forgot the time. They thought we'd got lost, and when they found us the coaches had been waiting ages!
> (*Evening Despatch*, 9 June 1937).

This day of independent enjoyment enabled by the Trust highlighted the noticeable shift from the highly-controlled approaches of the nineteenth century epitomised by the 1841 event celebrating the christening of the Princess Royal. Reflecting the class-biased language of the time, a newspaper stated that tea and plum cake were handed out to 126 residents at the Town Hall thanks to the 'genius' of the Bailiff, Thomas Ryland, who was blessed by the recipients of his bounty. The aged women sat down with "smiling faces and grateful minds presenting to the spectators a scene of interest eminently calculated to awaken the best sensibilities of the heart". There were also numerous ladies looking on, some of whom, at the request of the Bailiff, kindly consented to preside at the different tables. The shift away from the handing out of benevolence to 'inmates' and to a more inclusive and egalitarian approach to residents strengthened after the Second World War. (*Birmingham Journal*, 13 February 1841).

Chapter 11

Post-1945 Continuity and Change

With significant changes already affecting its historic estates in the older central wards of Birmingham, where the council was planning wholesale redevelopment, the Trustees decided to shift their focus to the outer city. In 1939, a year after the death of their long-standing Clerk, Arthur Musgrove, the Trustees put forward a new scheme. By then, there were 185 almswomen and 52 permanent and 38 temporary pensioners, but as in the past, Lench's favoured almshouses as a better way to assist needy women. Consequently, they wanted to sell those in Hospital Street and replace them with a new development in Ridgacre Road, Quinton.

After discussion with the Charity Commission, the scheme was adopted in late September, just weeks after the declaration of war with Nazi Germany. With the Government calling upon everyone to contribute to the war effort and with collections for military personnel, the War Comforts Fund appealed for donations to buy 50,000 cigarettes. Mrs. L. J. Owens of the Conybere Street almshouses responded, sending a postal order for 15 shillings and explaining that:

> I am an old Walsall woman, spent my first 50 years of life there. So am, of course, always interested, but cannot do much for them. I've saved over 11s. of the enclosed in halfpennies, and a few friends have made the amount for me. What a mad world this seems to be just now, but our leaders and brave lads are not finished with Hitler and his crowd of murderers. May God grant us an early and lasting peace.

Miss E. Robinson, "a very old pensioner", also sent a postal order for 6 pence, whilst Mrs. Owens posted another 11 shillings in March 1940 collected in halfpennies by herself and three other residents. She captured the thoughts of so many when longing for "peace in this troublesome world and our brave lads back home with their families and friends". It was an awful task for "all those responsible for our safety and I do think that we should all try and make that task as easy as possible, not harder by looking for mistakes, which are sure to be made. God bless and guide our leaders and guide our men to victory and a lasting peace". The 'old ladies' of Conybere Street later sent £5 10 shillings to another fund.

(*Birmingham Gazette*, 22 November 1939 and 30 March 1940 and *Birmingham Mail*, 24 June 1944).

Despite the outbreak of war, the Trustees pressed ahead with the building of the new almshouses in Ridgacre Road which were opened in the middle of 1940. As author and newspaper columnist Vivian Bird recognised, this was a bold decision, and it proved providential. With Birmingham a major centre of munitions production for the war effort, it was heavily targeted by the Luftwaffe and during an air raid in November 1940, the Hospital Street almshouses were bombed. Fortunately, nobody was killed but the residents had to be evacuated, although only half could be accommodated as Ridgacre Road was only partially completed. The Hospital Street site was bombed twice more and sold in 1943.

Lying as it also did in a heavily-blitzed industrial neighbourhood, the Conybere Street almshouses were hit and sadly, one resident was killed. Nearby in Ravenhurst Street, Selina Elizabeth Morgan was another victim. She died on the evening of 22/23 November when the enemy declared that "owing to the favourable weather all kinds of attacks could be carried out". Single raiders and mass formations followed each other, and though they concentrated on those armament works which hadn't yet been hit, it was admitted that as well as factories whole streets were destroyed and gutted by fire. (Vivian Bird, 'Birmingham Activities for the Common Weal', *Birmingham Weekly Post*, 10 February 1950 and 'German Version', *Birmingham Mail*, 23 November 1940 and 'Deaths', 29 November 1940).

Thankfully, the tide of war soon changed and the enemy was finally defeated in 1945. Seven years later, the Trust's income was £8,500 and there were 192 almswomen paying for normal living expenses but having a bed sitting room with cooking facilities rent free. As in the past, normally applications were accepted only from widows or spinsters of good character between the ages of 60 and 75 who'd been living in Birmingham for five years. Perhaps needing the help and comfort of people around her, that age range ensured that a woman had time to settle in and make friends before beginning to slow down seriously. When anyone became too infirm to fend for herself, usually she went to live with relatives who undertook to look after her. In such cases, the woman was granted a pension pending an enquiry into her circumstances. (*Birmingham Daily Post*, 13 January 1956).

Then in 1956, plans were drawn up for the modernisation of the homes in Conybere Street and Ladywood. Alterations were to follow at Ravenhurst Street, and it was hoped that more places would be built in Ridgacre Road. Those hopes were realised in 1963. As Lench's Trust qualified as a housing association, Birmingham Council gave it a £10,000 mortgage towards paying for a two-storey block of eight almshouses on the same lines as the existing five blocks at Ridgacre

A 1950s bedsitter room after modernisation.

Road. In addition, there were to be six single-storey almshouses to the south of the site. The council also agreed to 'pass on' the housing subsidy received from the Government, another boost towards the estimated cost of around £30,000.

The Lord Mayor, Alderman Dr. Louis Glass, officially opened the development on 11 October. Two spinsters who received keys were Hilda McMeel aged 65, a former bookkeeper, and 68-year-old Hilda Duckett, previously the bed bureau officer for Birmingham Regional Hospitals Board. They'd lived together in a first floor flat in Bournville which Hilda McMeel had difficulty getting up to because of a leg disability. She told a reporter, "This is heaven. We are delighted we can still live together. We each have our own bed sitting rooms but we are able to carry on sharing everyday living". (*Birmingham Daily Post*, 12 October 1963).

Ruth Richards was happy that as Bailiff, the increased number of Lench's homes was completed during her year of office. Her husband, Fred O. L. Richards was a former alderman on the council and one time Airport Committee Chairman, whilst she herself was a longstanding member of the Trust's Ladies' Committee and a Trustee for eight years. After the opening, she explained that

The Lord Mayor, Alderman Dr. Louis Glass, greeting 90-year-old Miss A Smith at the opening of the new Ridgacre Road almshouses in October 1963. Miss Smith presented a bouquet to the Lady Mayoress.

"Most of our capital is in property. We usually spend more than our income, but when we realise property we generally re-invest the money with the Charity Commissioners' Trust". (*Birmingham Mail*, 21 October 1963).

Throughout its history of providing almshouses, the Trust always had more applicants than it could accommodate. By 1971, that situation had changed, leading Barbara Crossette of the *Birmingham Daily Post* to ask, "Why 16 comfortable bedsitters are vacant?" She answered that accommodation for the elderly was now easier to find because of Birmingham's massive post-war programme of council housing and because people shied away quite unnecessarily from the name almshouse. However, the Trust's officers were convinced that word of available accommodation was not reaching those in need. The breaking down of neighbourhoods and the subsequent rearranging of lives had taken its toll on the old lines of communication. Notices in the press didn't have the desired effect and so, for the first time, bedsitters were empty.

A bedsitter room in about 1971.

This was despite the ideal accommodation for elderly women offered by Lench's. A resident overseer/matron for each set of almshouses was chosen, not for formal qualifications but for her ability to be kindly and understanding. She, and often her husband, were always on the premises, with the matron visiting each woman every morning to see that all was well. The residents were never isolated but neither were they badgered nor restricted by unnecessary interference. Each resident's room was her own and could be arranged as she liked so that each quickly took on the personality of its resident. Having her own key, each woman could come and go as she pleased. Her life, then, was a happy blend of privacy and individuality without loneliness. A spokesperson for the Trust noted that, "Many of our residents were women in service. Others were living with families that found as children grew up that there was no more room for grandmother". Still, "We believe there are women living in the poorer areas of this city whose standard of living we could raise". (Barbara Crossette, 'Why 16 comfortable bedsitters are vacant', *Birmingham Daily Post,* 27 October 1971).

A few weeks later, Miss McMeel's sister in Surrey wrote to the newspaper hoping that her observations might resolve the fears of any would-be residents in Lench's unique dwellings. For eight years, Hilda McMeel and her friend in an adjoining dwelling had lived happily at Ridgacre Road, enjoying the protection and comfort "due to the generosity and foresight of the originators of the Lench's Trust, and the present administrators". There was no sense whatsoever of either woman being in an 'institution'. On the contrary, the privacy, companionship and comfort found on visits gave the happiest memories. (*Birmingham Daily Post*, 17 November 1971).

The pace of change for Lench's now speeded up. In 1976, the Ravenshurst almshouses were sold for £30,000, leaving only those in Conybere Street and Ladywood from the nineteenth century. Now set amidst modernistic structures, it seemed to reporter Margaret Brown that these Ladywood homes crouched like Victorian dolls' houses at the foot of one of Birmingham's tallest office blocks.

> Yet despite their anachronistic appearance in a landscape of massive concrete and glass blocks and swirling traffic converging on Five Ways, they provide a form of community living which, as Canon Norman Power, Vicar of Ladywood says "is being copied by housing associations and the city all over the place.
>
> "I visit most of the old people there and I'm always impressed by the lively independent people I meet there. They certainly don't just sit watching telly all day".

The residents included Miss Florence Dunn, a former domestic hospital worker now in her late 70s, who received meals on wheels. Others shopped for those who couldn't get out. One of them was Mrs. Mary Smart, aged 77 and a former Edgbaston housekeeper, who said, "I prefer this to an old people's home. You can do what you like. I speak to everyone and run errands". Supervisor Mrs. Coral Furness lived on the premises. Checking on everyone each day, she was always at

Mrs. Coral Furness, matron of the Ladywood almshouses, with Mrs. Mary Smart, one of the residents in the once-secluded courtyard now overlooked by tower blocks on all sides. (Alan Hill, Birmingham Post, *10 January 1978, Thanks to the Birmingham Mail).*

hand if anyone needed anything, emphasising that "It's very happy. I can't speak too highly of the Lench's Trust". (Margaret Brown, 'Community among the tower blocks', *Birmingham Daily Post*, 10 January 1978).

Speaking on behalf of the Trust, clerk Mr. David Lowe noted that it was in the process of changing from its 1882 scheme. If the Charity Commissioners agreed, residents might be asked for contributions towards rent. It was also hoped that henceforth, both men and women would be admitted. In anticipation of this major shift in policy, work would soon begin on new almshouses off the Wake Green Road in Moseley which would include accommodation for married couples. Built to a high specification around a traditional village green, final contracts for the aptly named Lench's Close were signed in July 1979, with a projected cost of £750,000 and an opening in 1981.

A sheltered housing scheme, one of its residents was Larry Farrington, a childhood friend of my father, Buck Chinn. I knew Larry well as he used to bet with us when we were bookmakers on the Ladypool Road and he was the manager of a car sales pitch on the corner of the Stratford Road and Long Street. A great friend of Eddie Fewtrell, the man who brought nightclubs to Birmingham, Larry

A July garden fete, organised by Birmingham pensioners, raised more than £1,100 for St Mary's Hospice, Selly Oak. A cheque for £1,152.28 was presented by Mrs Edith Austin (left), of Lenches Close Sheltered Housing Accommodation, Moseley, to founder of the hospice, Miss Monica Pearce. Looking on, Mrs Jan Monk (right) deputy warden of the hospice, Mrs Birdie Ceaser (second right) warden and residents.

Birmingham Mail, *15 August 1988; thanks to the* Birmingham Mail.

was a larger-than-life character who valued his tenancy at Lench's Close in the latter years of his life.

Other residents at Lench's Close were prominent in raising funds for a variety of worthy causes. Garden fêtes in 1987 and 1988 brought in £340 and over £1,100 respectively for St. Mary's Hospice and in 1991, residents took part in a 'Walk the World for Schizophrenia' in Cannon Hill Park. In 1995, through another walk, they made £540 for the MacMillan Appeal, although they didn't appreciate a local newspaper describing them as living in an old folks' home. Responding through Mrs. Walton, the Residents' Committee registered their irritation at the patronising few lines:

> This is not an old folks' home ... we all have our own flats and look after ourselves with the watchful eye and help of the warden at all times. The average age of the walkers was certainly around 80 years but all enjoyed the fun of the walk and the tea afterwards both of which were part of our VE Day celebrations. It was a very good effort on the part of a group of people who deserve a better description than "old folks". Pensioners, OAP's, Senior Citizens – any of these would sound more flattering. (*Birmingham News*, 1 June 1995).

A few days after this retort, on 13 June 1995, Her Royal Highness the Duchess of Gloucester unveiled a commemorative plaque at the Trust's new Tanner's Close Sheltered Housing Scheme, off Whitehouse Common Road in

On 13 June 1995, Her Royal Highness the Duchess of Gloucester unveiled a commemorative plaque at the Trust's new Tanner's Close Sheltered Housing Scheme, off Whitehouse Common Road in Sutton Coldfield. Here five-year-old Maria, the daughter of Marion O'Mara the warden, is presenting flowers to the Duchess.

Sutton Coldfield. Recalling the occupation of William Lenche, it was a £1 million development of 24 self-contained flats opened in September 1993 for single men and women and couples needing safe and warm homes. On her arrival, the Duchess was greeted by the Clerk, Jenny McGowran, builder Ken Jones, and Paul Burley the architect and given a guided tour of the flats and the facilities. A highlight was the presentation of a bouquet of flowers by five-year-old Maria, the daughter of Marion O' Mara the warden, who said that, "The Duchess of Gloucester was very nice, she was very pleasant and relaxed with us and she was interested in the scheme and the people who lived there. The residents loved it and thoroughly enjoyed the visit". (*Sutton Coldfield Observer*, 16 June 1995).

The Clerk, Jenny McGowran, took advantage of the royal visit to publicise not only the Trust's history but also its place in modern Birmingham. Noting that the question of the repairs and updating of the properties was a priority for the Trust, she took heating as an example: "In small flats or bed-sitters open fires have become almost obsolete. We have had to get rid of our coal cupboards and install central heating". In a programme started after the Second World War, almshouses were now equipped with bathrooms and adequate cooking facilities, whilst some of the later developments even had communal rooms where residents could meet.

Importantly, the Trust had taken on responsibilities for the aged and infirm: "We now have to employ outside help in addition to our wardens. A bath lady for instance. Many elderly people find bathing increasingly difficult". So too was shopping for everything from food to picking up prescriptions and so the Trust also took on those responsibilities. If the resident was able to pay rent, a charge of around £42 per week was made, but anyone unable to pay received state help. Having maintained its commitment to the needy, Lench's had also adapted to the needs of modern society and once again, the waiting list was always growing. Proud of the Trust's achievements, Jenny McGowran linked the past with the present: "William Lenche probably has no idea of the benefit he has given to the citizens of Birmingham over almost 500 years. Nor the continuing need we are trying to stem". (Christine Barker, 'Trusting in a Tudor legacy', *Birmingham Post*, 13 June 1995).

Along with its commitment to helping the needy, that link with the past is a constant in Lench's history but crucially, it's matched by the recognition that a changing society requires changing approaches. From the late 1990s, the Trust advertised itself as an equal opportunities organisation and its commitment to equality is bolstered by its awareness of the changing demographics of Birmingham and the importance of inclusivity and diversity. Those can be challenges but they are challenges to which the Trust has responded positively in the twenty first century.

Chapter 12

The Nineties, Noughties, and Now

Dominic Bradley, Chief Executive, Lench's Trust

Post the development of Tanner's Close in 1993, it was a challenging period financially for the Trust, with the Ladywood and Conybere almshouses needing subsidy year on year as they became loss-making assets. The prevailing view taken at the time by the Trustees and Management was that the loss was partly due to the areas in which the schemes were located and, perhaps more significantly, that all the schemes were either bedsits or very small and compact compared to more modern developments. All of this rightly meant that our properties were becoming less desirable for older people, despite the

A photograph of the Conybere almshouses in Highgate.

exceptionally low rents. Alongside the major council building programme, which included numerous larger sheltered housing schemes, many housing associations developed more modern, spacious, and desirable accommodation for older people throughout the '80s, '90s and '00s.

The year 2000/01 was the Trust's 475th birthday and Charles Gillet, a member of the Cadbury family, was Bailiff. This birthday event was celebrated with a residents' tea party at the Botanical Gardens, with the Lord Mayor in attendance, and a church service at St. Martin's Church in the Bull Ring, where a plaque to William Lench is on display. The Trust began several asset disposals during this period with the sale of a commercial property on Bristol Road South in Northfield in 2001 for £85,000. This was followed by land on the Stratford Road and Gladstone Road on the Sparkbrook Estate in April and October 2003 for a combined total of £3,500.

Then in 2004, the Trustees made the difficult decision to sell a long 150-year leasehold interest on the Ladywood almshouses to a private developer. The scheme has proved popular with young professionals due to its proximity to the city centre, with work, social life, and amenities all within walking distance from its location on the ever busy Five Ways Island.

In the mid-'80s, it was decided to sell a building located next to Lench's Close on Wake Green Road (in the conservation area of Moseley Village), which had been unused for a few years. DTZ, who gave professional advice to the Trust, advised to board it up and when inspected a few years later, the building was deemed too expensive to refurbish. After the sale, it underwent significant refurbishment and was used as offices. The Trustees also authorised the sale of an office property in central Lichfield, 28 Market Street, to boost the financial position of the Trust and it was sold on 4 December 2003 for over £400,000.

Conybere Gardens was the next to go, but interestingly, a different approach was taken by the Trust in its disposal. Due to its listed status and location in the heart of Highgate, it proved difficult to sell outright. Conybere Gardens was eventually leased to St. Basil's, a significant local young people's charity and housing association. The lease began on the 2 December 2005. St. Basil's is now in its 20th year of leasing Conybere Gardens from the Trust, with the most recent extension of the lease completed in 2024.

It is possible that inspiration was drawn from Lench's other almshouse in Highgate, Ravenhurst Cottages, which, since its sale by the Trust in 1976, had been used as student accommodation. However, it returned to its social-purpose roots in 1997 when it was purchased by Trident Housing Association for £500,000 and refurbished with support from the Housing Corporation into 33 bedsits for young people at risk of homelessness. Ravenhurst Cottages became the first accredited Foyer in Birmingham. The Foyer movement was originally a

A recent photograph of the Conybere almshouses, now known as Conybere Gardens, leased to St. Basil's since 2005.

French concept, with the overriding philosophy being that the accommodation for young homeless people had to be more than a roof over someone's head. This meant that the accommodation offer was supplemented with direct links to education, training, and employment, with the idea that positive social networks and economic independence are the most sustainable routes out of the cycle of homelessness. Both Conybere and Ravenhurst remain in use for young people at risk of homelessness to this day, breathing new life and an important new social use into the Trust's almshouses.

A photograph of the Ravenhurst Cottages.

Jane Rudge, the CEO during this challenging period, left the Trust in late 2005, and Derek Dyas, who was a Trustee with vast social housing management experience, became the acting CEO until the appointment of Jean-Luc Priez in May 2006. Jean-Luc was an interesting and dynamic appointment as his previous roles had been within hospices with no prior experience in social housing or the almshouse movement. That notwithstanding, Jean-Luc began his tenure with a clear remit to instil financial stability. The Trust was running out of land and buildings to sell, and its remaining almshouses needed to move from loss-making to at least break-even if the Trust was to remain viable for the long term. As the Trustees noted at the time, the reserves wouldn't last forever, and the Trust's investment properties and banking investments were subsidising its operations at an unsustainable level.

The immediacy of the challenges was laid bare with the Ridgacre site, where the apartments, which were no longer bedsits but very small, were now deemed undesirable by potential residents, just as Ravenhurst, Conybere and Ladywood had been a decade before. Interestingly the newest built scheme, Tanner's Close, was loss-making and the issue was simmering in the background, with Trustees and management noting concerns as to the scheme's viability.

A photograph of Tanner's Close from the team at Creative Bridge.

This was not because of empty properties – Tanner's had always been very popular, with a substantial waiting list. However, despite this, the Trust was subsiding every single apartment within the trust to the tune of £12 to £20 per week. During the 2009/10 financial year, after challenging discussions with Trustees, it was agreed that work was needed on the weekly maintenance charges, and the accommodation class changed to supported exempt accommodation at Lench's Close and Tanner's Close. This allowed some of the service charges that the Trust was subsidising to be included in the maintenance charges and thus eligible for housing benefit. This was common practice amongst most later living/older people providers in the social housing sector and was so since 2003, with the introduction of the supported people regime under the office of the Deputy Prime Minister (Labour's John Prescott). However, this approach was less prevalent in the more traditional almshouse movement, and the decision was not taken lightly by the Trust. A fund was set aside by the Trustees to financially assist those residents receiving only partial housing benefit who were affected by the increase in maintenance charges. The principle around financial hardship support remains in place to the present day.

This put in place a solid platform, meaning that Tanner's Close was no longer subsidised by the Trust. The one remaining hurdle was Ridgacre Road, where the small apartments were causing an issue with vacancies that could not be filled. To give some perspective of the living conditions, in the bedrooms, you could have either a bed or a wardrobe, never both! This meant that wardrobes were frequently placed in the living room or corridor, often found next to the fridge! The only solution was a further reduction in the number of apartments to make the apartments bigger. The costs associated with this proposal were over £2

The Ridgacre almshouses before the William Lench Court Extra Care scheme was constructed.

million. At face value, this premise did not have a strong business case, given the additional loss of apartments. However, a number of the Trustees were keen to pursue this option, and many of the Trustees had a strong relationship with the Trust architect who had designed the scheme. Jean-Luc advised that he thought this was not a good use of the Trust's resources and so he was tasked with producing a strategy and options appraisal for the Ridgacre site.

Jean-Luc instructed Charles Cox, an architect he knew from his previous role, to review the plans and together they worked on looking at the possibility of designing an extra care scheme – a radical alternative to the existing proposal. Jean-Luc presented the board with three options: do nothing (which was already broadly agreed as unsustainable); modernise with an overall reduction in units (apartments); or knock down the existing Ridgacre almshouses and build a new extra care scheme. The third option featured a scheme design that incorporated all the main principles of extra care, with the overriding aim being for people to live independently, but with the peace of mind of having on-site care workers to help when it was needed, 24/7. The scheme design included a café/bistro, lounge, activity rooms, hair salon, and extensive gardens.

However the options appraisal caused significant disagreement among the Trustees on the best course of action. While there was universal agreement that continuing the status quo was not an option, there was a split, with some supporting the more radical extra care proposal and some preferring the modernisation of the existing accommodation. Importantly, Jean-Luc had the

Former trustee James Lloyd (left) with other Trustees enjoying a lunch in the 80s.

support of the Bailiff, Christine Kenrick, who was a Trustee for over 30 years and whose family had been involved in the Trust for many years. James Lloyd, who was the Chair of the Finance Committee, also supported Jean-Luc. James was from the Lloyds banking family and had been a Trustee since 1971, following in the footsteps of his father and forebearers in the nineteenth century. Between them, the Lloyd/Chamberlain families accumulated over 100 years' service to the Trust.

Jean-Luc was tasked with presenting a business case for the extra care proposal. The main opposition were longstanding Trustees, all of whom felt that the Extra Care proposal could be financially disastrous for the Trust. Despite the reservations from a few prominent Trustees, the Extra Care proposal was agreed in principle in July 2006 (subject to the financial appraisal/business case). However, between November 2006 and September 2007, half of the Trustees resigned in protest, including the newly-appointed Bailiff and former acting CEO. One key reason for this was what the Trustees termed the Martineau Doctrine (named after a previous Trustee, Denis Martineau). According to this doctrine, all interests from investments had to be re-invested in the existing portfolio, and all receipts of sale of lands/properties had to be invested likewise, effectively ruling out the possibility of a new-build scheme.

Despite this, the remaining Trustees held their nerve and continued to work on the business case for the Extra Care proposal. Gaining support from Birmingham City Council proved difficult. The responsibility for social care at the time was under the direction of Peter Hay and Elaine Elkington was responsible for the housing element, both of whom needed convincing to support the Trust's proposal. It was eventually included as a pipeline scheme and received the strategic support it required for grant funding from the Homes and Communities Agency, HCA.

It wasn't until 2010, four years after the initial seismic meetings with the Trustees, that a spade was put in the ground as the demolition began, following the successful rehousing of all the existing Ridgacre residents. Due to the Trust's concerns about its financial capacity to build a scheme comprising of 95 apartments, it was agreed – unusually for a scheme of this nature – that the development would be built in two phases. The scheme was to be named after the founder, namely William Lench Court.

The first phase was completed in 2011 and developed with support from Waterloo Housing Association as the preferred partner with the HCA. Mansell's was appointed as the main builder after an extensive tendering exercise. Funding came from the HCA, a capital appeal, the sale of the Trust's head office on the Hagley Road, the charity's reserves, the proceeds of the 21 shared ownership sales, and two separate loans from Lloyds Bank – one for each phase of the

William Lench Court, phase 2, construction in progress.

development totalling £5.8 million (£1.8 million for phase 1 and £4 million for phase 2). The total scheme cost came in at £9.2 million and provided the Trust with 95 apartments in total. This is one of very few almshouse developments offering shared ownership to meet the needs of owner-occupiers who cannot afford outright ownership.

The Housing Our Ageing Population: Panel for Innovation (HAPPI) was established in June 2009 to consider what is needed to ensure that new-build specialised housing meets the needs and aspirations of the older people of the future. Their report outlined innovative housing examples from across Europe and made recommendations to central and local government, and developers. The All-Party Parliamentary Group (APPG) on Housing and Care for Older People, chaired by Lord Best, highlighted the benefits of improved housing options for older people in their HAPPI2 report and plan for implementation (2012).

The Trust interpreted 'need' in the twenty first century as encompassing health, social, or housing needs, as well as the financial need of the applicants. William Lench Court at the Ridgacre site was designed as a community hub, with extensive communal facilities.

Phase 1 included 63 one- and two-bedroom apartments; the scheme was fully occupied within a year of completion. Nineteen apartments across the site are occupied by shared owners. It was agreed that two apartments (with HCA agreement) could be used flexibly for shared ownership or lettings. The 'rental' element of the shared ownership lease is a licence, not a tenancy, which is an important distinction for almshouses, and it was approved by both the Charity Commission and the HCA. Most shared owners bought a 50% share, though shares range from 25% to 75%. Lench's Trust had partnerships with two other charities: first with Yardley Great Trust (also a historical Birmingham-based almshouse charity and registered with the Care Quality Commission) which provided the Home Care Team, offering help with personal care and domestic tasks to court residents and to local people in the wider community. All staff were recruited and trained by YGT; staff were directly employed. The Jericho Foundation, a local social enterprise, initially ran the café-restaurant. Jericho provides training and employment to people from disadvantaged backgrounds and minority ethnic groups, through a number of social enterprises.

William Lench Court officially opened in May 2011, and the first residents were Mr. and Mrs. Bridgwater, who moved in on 16 May 2011. Mr. Bridgwater still lives at William Lench Court, his wife sadly passed away several years prior.

Phase 2, which comprised of 32 additional one- and two-bedroom apartments and a new eco-pod to be used as the head office, officially opened in 2016. The lead builder was Manton's, and the official opening was conducted by David Orr, the Chief Executive of the National Housing Federation.

David Orr giving a speech at the grand opening at William Lench Court with many familiar faces including Jean-Luc Priez, Charles Cox, Tina Swani, Jayne McGettrick and Dominic Bradley to name a few!

William Lench Court has proved to be a huge success for the Trust. The main changes that have taken place since the original opening include bringing the care in-house in 2014, following the Trust registering with the Care Quality Commission, which was followed by bringing the catering service in-house in 2015. Both decisions were made to improve the resident experience of these services. Since taking the Care service in-house, it has been inspected by CQC and rated as "Good" after inspection and monitoring visits. The hygiene rating since the Trust taking on responsibility for the café/restaurant is a 5, the highest rating available.

Visitors at the new head office grand opening at William Lench Court.

Following the prompt resignations of many Trustees early in Jean-Luc's tenure, a greater focus on diversity and skills became a driver for Trustee recruitment. Shihab Hussain was appointed by the Trust after partnering with the Asian Institute of Business (part of the Chamber of Commerce), as was Tina Swani, who latterly became Bailiff and was fundamental in changing this traditional almshouse archaic term to Chair of the Board during her tenure. Tina remained part of the almshouse movement post her involvement as a Trustee at Lench's, and she went on to became CEO of the Sutton Coldfield Charitable Trust, leaving that role in early 2025.

The Trust adopted the National Housing Federation Code of Governance, which meant that Trustee tenure is limited to between six to nine years maximum. To maintain skills on the Board, it was decided by Trustees that the Chair only serves a two-year term of office and then steps down to become a Trustee. This approach keeps skills, knowledge, and relationships intact, whilst also providing invaluable support for the new Chair. It has proved to be an invaluable tool within Lench's governance and management of the Trust.

A small working party, led by a Trustee, was established to discuss the sale of phase 1 of the historic St. Mary's Estate (Lancaster Gate). It took many years to secure the right offer from a developer, with the financial crash in 2008 intervening during critical negotiations. However, a sale on a long leasehold was finally realised in 2018 for £7 million, with a RPI linked ground rent of £120,000 per annum. The site now houses the imposing Onyx building, a huge black tower. This purpose-built student accommodation consists of 1,025 bedrooms spread across two tower blocks of 13 and 24 storeys. Achieving a Building Research Establishment Environmental Assessment Method (BREEAM) 'Excellent' rating, the development boasts views of Birmingham's 'Gun Quarter' and beyond, cementing itself as an opinion-splitting landscape icon.

The sale gave the Trust much-needed funds, allowing Lench's to invest significantly in its existing schemes and homes. This included creating accessible apartments, fitting dormers, upgrading schemes offices, resurfacing car parks to include barrier access, upgrading bathrooms and kitchens, and replacing all the fire doors. The replacement of fire doors was an important and significant investment following the Grenfell fire tragedy, which has cast a long shadow over social housing. The sale enabled the Trust to get the best-in-class fire-rated doors, which cost in excess of half a million pounds alone.

Phase 2 of Lancaster Gate is still being developed, with a longstop date of 2036 for the expiration of an existing lease on the old Fonz Leather site. However, the Trust is currently negotiating with the current leaseholder to develop the site or buy out the leasehold interest. In 2024, the Trust purchased 90 Lancaster Street for £1.26 million from Midland Heart with a leaseback arrangement.

The site was originally a clinic but has operated as a supported housing scheme for homeless men and, more recently, as social housing. It comprises 15 apartments with communal areas. Interestingly, the building features sculptures on the outside by the renowned local artist William Bloye, who played a significant role as Birmingham's unofficial civic sculptor, contributing to various public commissions, most famously the gilded bronze statue of Boulton, Watt and Murdoch on Broad Street.

In 2018, Lench's also took on the responsibility of three grant-making Trusts:

The Walker Pensions Fund

This fund was established via the will of Mrs. Emily Louisa Walker in 1938. The initial object was to assist, by way of pensions, gifts or otherwise, aged or distressed persons (male or female) professing the Protestant faith and belonging to the upper or middle classes of society, provided that such persons had been reduced to poverty by misfortune and not their own improvidence or neglect. Special regards had to be paid to the claims of widows and daughters of clergymen of the Church of England.

Catherine Cornforth Charity

The fund was established by the will of Mrs. Catherine Cornforth in 1908, with the object of assisting male or female residents of Birmingham or within a radius of five miles from the Town Hall and who were in indigent circumstances and over the age of 55.

Persehouse Pension Funds

This fund was established by the will of Henry Persehouse Parkes in 1900, with the objectives similar to the Walker Pensions Fund: assisting by way of pensions or otherwise, aged or distressed persons (male or female) belonging to the upper or middle classes of society who were natives of Staffordshire or Worcestershire, or who had for 10 years or upwards bona fide resided in one or other of these counties, provided that such persons shall have been reduced to poverty by misfortune and not by their own improvidence or neglect. Pensions were granted for one year and renewed annually at the sole discretion of the Trustees.

The purpose of the grants has naturally evolved over time with the onerous and discriminatory conditions removed and they remain a key part of the Lench's support for the wider communities of Birmingham, Staffordshire, and Worcestershire. (The descriptions above contain some of the original language of the time).

The last properties to be sold by the Trust were two small houses on Maas Road in Northfield, originally gifted to the Trust in 2007. They were sold in 2013 and 2014, after the existing residents moved out, as the properties were deemed unsuitable for older people at the point of sale. One couple moved into William Lench Court, and the other occupant was the retired Warden from Ridgacre Road who moved to be closer to her family in Devon.

The Trust navigated the ongoing challenges of the financial crash, the austerity which followed, the biggest welfare reforms since the post-war period, Brexit and the uncertainty this created in the economy, and the short and economically disastrous premiership of Liz Truss. However, the most challenging period for the Trust was undoubtedly the COVID-19 pandemic. The effect on residents was profound, with social isolation being a hugely significant factor. Thankfully, the spread of COVID-19 among the vulnerable older client group was managed exceptionally well. During one of the lockdowns, the Trust courted controversy with a national newspaper picking up on signage displayed by the Trust at William Lench Court, which was considered alarmist and draconian.

In June 2023, after 17½ largely successful years at the helm, Jean-Luc retired, leaving the Trust in robust financial health, all the Trust's properties in excellent condition, a stable management team in place, and excellent frontline teams. Jean-Luc was replaced by Dominic Bradley, who ironically started his career in a Lench's-built building at Ravenhurst Cottages in 2002 as a support worker for Trident Housing Association.

Dominic Bradley introducing himself for the first time to residents at staff at William Lench Court, with his predecessor Jean-Luc alongside him.

In 2024, planning permission and listed-building consent was gained for Conybere Gardens, however plans to bring them back into the Trust's management were shelved due to concerns of the rising cost of the development which was estimated close to £5 million to create 21 new apartments.

Plans were also shelved to knock down the old warden's house at Tanner's Close and replace it with four apartments, as the costs came in at over £1 million. After consultation with existing residents, key agencies, and Trustees, the decision was made to convert the old warden's house to a co-living environment called Marion's Place. This opened in January 2025 and the scheme was named after Marion O'Mara, the former scheme manager. Marion had lived in the house with her husband and children since the scheme opened in 1993. Unfortunately, Marion passed away in 2022 after a long illness and 29 years' service to the Trust and the house remained empty.

The Lord Mayor, Councillor John Alden with late Scheme Manager Marion O'Mara (left) at the Town Hall.

This is Lench's first co-living project, and the accommodation is aimed at older people who may be experiencing social isolation, need additional care and support, or simply prefer living with other people. The house has been refurbished into a homely, co-living space for three people. Good housing conditions can help to sustain good physical and mental health, particularly for an age group exposed to loneliness and social isolation. More than 3.5 million older people in the UK live alone (Age UK), this is thought to increase the likelihood of dementia or depression among an already vulnerable age group. Marion's family were engaged in the refurbishment of the house and Marion's husband Gary, who still lives in a Lench's property, helped with the signage for Marion's Place.

There are many chapters still to be written, with plans afoot to grow the Trust in the coming years. At the time of writing, the Trust has 186 units of accommodation, 200 residents, and 59 staff serving our own residents and the wider citizens of Birmingham and beyond.

A proud history and a story that will be continued. As the twenty first century unfolds, our society will continue to change. Lench's Trust will continue engaging with Birmingham's future generation of older people who are facing financial hardship or social isolation. Work is already afoot that will hopefully be in the next chapter on a new model of modern almshouses, these include multi-generational living proposals and planning in process for a unique Eco-Pod Scheme to support wellbeing and nature connectivity amongst our city's working elders.

A story to be continued.

Sources

Primary

Catherine Hutton Beale, *Memorials of the Old Meeting House and Burial Ground Birmingham* (1882).

W. B. Bickley (translated), *A Survey of the Manor of Birmingham made in the 1st year of Queen Mary, 1553* (c.1890).

W. B. Bickley (transcribed & edited), 'The Register of the Guild of Knowle in the County of Warwick, 1451-1535: From the Original' (1894).

Birmingham Archives, Heritage and Photography Service, 'Further Records of Lench's Trust' (14th cent. – 18th cent.).

Censuses, 1841-1939.

Jacqueline B. Geater, *Birmingham Wills and Inventories 1512-1603* (2016).

Joseph Hill, *Unpublished Records relating to Birmingham* (1892).

Jens Röhrkasten (ed.), *The Warwickshire Eyre Roll of 1262* (2022).

Lucy Toulmin Smith, *Lench's Trust. Copies of the Original Deeds upon which it rests, and of those upon which it is now administered* (1869).

Staffordshire, Dioceses of Lichfield and Coventry Wills and Probate 1521-1860.

'The Public Charities of Birmingham', *Aris's Birmingham Gazette* 14, 21, and 28 December 1829 and 4 January 1830).

Secondary

George Demidowicz, *Medieval Birmingham: The Borough Rentals of 1296 and 1344-45* (2008).

R. K. Dent, *Old and New Birmingham. A History of the Town and its People. Section 3* (1880).

William Dugdale, *The Antiquities of Warwickshire* (1656).

Conrad Gill. 'Birmingham in the Sixteenth Century', in, *Studies in Midland History* (1930).

Joseph Hill, 'The Old Families of Birmingham' in *Transactions of the Birmingham and Warwickshire Archaeological Society* (1885).

Richard Holt, *The Early History of the Town of Birmingham, 1166 to 1600* (1985).

Arthur Musgrove, *The History of Lench's Trust Birmingham, 1525-1925* (1926).

Joshua Toulmin Smith, *English Guilds* (1870).